Napoleon Hill's
Magic Ladder to Success

A Commentary on the Ideas and Vision of
The Bestselling Author of
Think and Grow Rich
The Law of Success
How to Sell your Way Through Life
Master Key to Riches
Success Through a Positive Mental Attitude
Grow Rich With Peace of Mind
You Can Work Your Own Miracles
PMA Science of Success Course

ISBN: 978-0-9838111-2-1

Published by The Napoleon Hill Foundation
PO Box 1277
Wise, Virginia 24293
Website: www.naphill.org
Email: napoleonhill@uvawise.edu

Contents

NAPOLEON HILL'S MAGIC LADDER TO SUCCESS

Introduction

Just what does a man born during the heyday of Chester A. Arthur have to teach us about success today? What makes Napoleon Hill a useful guide for people living in the twenty-first century? How can someone twenty-five years older than the Model T Ford shed any light on the struggle for success in the modern world?

Millions of people in every major country on earth have based their plans for success on the writings of a farmer's son born in backwoods Virginia more than 120 years ago. It's astonishing, really, that a fellow of such modest beginnings would have such an enduring influence, at least until one becomes familiar with the man and his ideas.

Napoleon Hill was a prolific writer. In addition to nearly a dozen books, he wrote and edited several magazines published out of New York and Chicago. He lectured across America over the course of forty years, and he was the subject of a documentary film and countless newspaper and magazine features. He certainly found an audience and provided it with plenty of material to digest. But this productivity is simply a sign of his influence, not the cause. He kept writing because people wanted to hear from him.

Napoleon Hill based his ideas about what makes a person successful on a long, twenty-odd-year investigation. He interviewed people who had changed the world, people who were universally acknowledged as having done what they wanted to do. He also, in the course of his research, met many more people who had failed to do what they wanted to do. And from the lives of these successes and failures, he distilled a philosophy of success based on an understanding of human nature.

This approach was fairly novel. Down through the ages, human beings have created belief systems to explain to themselves how the world works. But unlike Plato or Descartes or John Stuart Mill, Napoleon Hill did not begin with the question of what was good or right and then shape his ideas about humanity around these propositions. He began with the question of what made a person a success, and by careful observation, set forth a framework for others to follow in the pursuit of their own success.

Napoleon Hill was not the very first to take this path. Nicolo Machiavelli's famous work of political advice, *The Prince*, was based on gimlet-eyed pragmatism that has been admired and condemned since the fourteenth century. But unlike Machiavelli, Napoleon Hill was concerned with the personal, not the political, and his own findings were inspirational, not ruthless. A successful person, he discovered, creates more success, and in becoming happy and contented, creates more happiness and contentment.

This idea contrasted with ideas that were popular in the early twentieth century. Communism was raging through Europe. America still had a clear memory of the legendary robber barons who had used railroads to enrich themselves and ruin their competitors, men like James Fisk, who had made and lost a fortune through stock manipulation and ended up being shot in a duel over a woman. There was a strong suspicion that success was something wrung out of life by any method necessary, and the devil take the hindmost. Charles Darwin's theories of evolution, crudely boiled down to the idea of survival of the fittest, implied that only a few people would ever truly prosper, while the vast majority would be ground up and used as fodder for the dreams of the ruthless.

In a sense, what Napoleon Hill did was to reassert the possibility of the American Dream: you could, by dint of hard work and a vision of what you wanted, better yourself. His ideas were not limited to a single pathway: a salesman, a schoolteacher, a rabbi or an engineer could all apply Hill's thinking and be better off for it. And of course, many decades later, you still can.

The Ladder to Success was Napoleon Hill's second book. Originally published in 1930, it was essentially a greatly abridged version of Hill's national bestseller, *The Law of Success.* While *The Law of Success* has been almost constantly in print since its inception, *The Ladder* has been long out of print, overshadowed by its highly praised predecessor. As such, *The Ladder* presents an unusual opportunity that the Napoleon Hill Foundation has decided to explore in an effort to make clear just how useful and important Dr. Hill's philosophy of success has been.

Other early Napoleon Hill books have been reissued in updated editions since the early 1990s. These revisions have replaced outdated examples with fresh stories of modern successes; the likes of John Wanamaker and W.R. Wrigley have been succeeded by Bill Gates and Mary Kay Ash. Dr. Hill's analogies from the realm of science have turned from a discussion of the "ether" to string theory. Women and minorities have become a part of the audience for Dr. Hill's books, a change that would have delighted him endlessly. All these changes were made in the interest of revealing just how pertinent this philosophy of success remains long after it was first set down on paper.

Yet a reader who pours over the original text of an

early Napoleon Hill book comes away with something that cannot be gained from a modern edition: a sense of Dr. Hill's vision of the potential for advancement in human society and just how remarkably that vision has come to pass. One reads his technological predictions with amazement. The opportunities he saw for new enterprises are still being exploited today. And his ideas themselves have entered into the American consciousness so deeply that they are reflected everywhere, from the works of modern motivational writers to the arts and social sciences.

The unaltered text of this small book offers, therefore, a remarkable chance to explore and discuss the ways that Napoleon Hill's ideas remain viable and influential. The purpose of this examination is not to glorify Dr. Hill, but to aid people who are attempting to employ his philosophy in pursuit of their own dreams. Readers who are already familiar with the Seventeen Principles will recognize Imagination as an invaluable tool for creating a successful life. This edition of *The Ladder of Success* is intended as a spur to Imagination, a starting point to explore areas of your own life where Dr. Hill's ideas have relevance and power.

We will try to provoke you. We want you to think. We want you to reason things through, to struggle to make connections, and to examine old assumptions. You have not purchased just another Napoleon Hill book. You have purchased a book designed to make every other Napoleon Hill book you own exponentially more valuable.

This will happen when you participate in the dialog that follows. The questions that will be raised and the points that will be made are all chosen to fire up your Imagination and rejuvenate your passion for success. Indeed, Napoleon

Hill has nothing to say to someone who has stopped listening, and we want to get you to listen in a new way to what he has to say.

This book will be unlike any Napoleon Hill book you have ever read, and if you have not read Dr. Hill's word before this, we know that you will soon be eager to find out all you can about this man and his ideas. But the real test of the effectiveness of our experiment will lie not in whether you read more of Napoleon Hill. It will lie in whether you *apply* his ideas and begin to transform your life.

Are you ready to begin that process?

How This Book Works

This new edition of *The Ladder of Success* excerpts substantial portions of the original text and presents them with commentary designed to stimulate your thinking about Napoleon Hill's ideas. Each chapter will begin with a very general summary of the ideas that will be discussed. For newcomers to Napoleon Hill's ideas, this summary will provide a basic framework that will be filled in as the chapter progresses.

Readers who already know Dr. Hill's ideas may be tempted to skip over these summaries, but we caution against this. Important themes will be underscored and ways of thinking advanced that may be just what you need to begin applying the Seventeen Principles in ways that you have not yet done. Little will be gained by haste.

Occasionally, we will also excerpt text from other Napoleon Hill writings to amplify a point or to raise an issue that Dr. Hill had not addressed in the original *The Ladder of Success*. Dr. Hill remained an active speaker and writer for more than thirty years following the publication of this book, and he never stopped looking for new implications of his ideas. Personal successes and disappointments followed the appearance of *The Ladder of Success* and Dr. Hill's experiences only enriched his ability to see how people create their own fortunes.

Keep in mind that the style of this book's text belongs to a different era. Repetition was considered a good way to help readers remember what they had read. Italics were used liberally, and prose was more flowery. Spelling is occasionally different.

The rhetoric of the day did not include gender-specific pronouns that credited both men and women, but just because Dr. Hill uses male pronouns such as "salesmen" does not mean that he thought women had nothing to gain from his ideas. His newsletters frequently featured contributions about success from women. Dr. Hill understood the value of women's ideas, as should his readers

You may find that some of Dr. Hill's examples and suggestions don't fit with your ideas of success and how it is achieved. Our goal here has been to demonstrate just how widely applicable Dr. Hill's ideas are. If you encounter an idea and think, "That's not how I'd do it," fine. If you're satisfied that you are progressing toward your great ambition, you can disregard what you read. There is no single path to success. But, please, keep in mind that we are not showing you how to be successful: we are simply trying to stimulate your thinking on this subject. Stop yourself from thinking, resist evaluating what you encounter, and you will soon find that you have stopped yourself from doing much at all.

This does not mean you have to accept the commentary presented here as gospel. Only you know whether you are making satisfactory progress toward your goal in life. If you are, don't throw out your plan in order to try ideas you read here that run counter to your intuition and experience. Consider new ideas carefully, and if you decide they are not for you, don't spend a lot of time on second thoughts. What works for a high-powered investment banker may not be the best choice for a career military officer or a lawyer starting a practice.

Ideally, even ideas that are clearly not for you will inspire you to consider new possibilities and to evaluate old practices. It may be that you're doing nothing wrong; it's just that there is more that you could be doing right. An open mind to what your life can become is all you need to make your visions into reality.

Lesson One
THE MASTER MIND

SUMMARY

Napoleon Hill begins *The Ladder of Success* by explaining the Master Mind very succinctly:

The Master Mind principle may be defined as "A composite mind, consisting of two or more individual minds working in perfect harmony, with a definite aim in view."

Stated another way, the Master Mind is an extra mental force that is created when a group of people is so united in pursuit of a goal that they operate without conflict. This force is powerful, but fragile; it collapses when sustained friction occurs between contributors. This makes it a somewhat high-maintenance tool, but the benefits it brings are very worthwhile.

The Master Mind was an idea unique to Napoleon Hill in motivational literature. He saw it as something greater than the sum of its parts. That is, it combines the strengths of the participants and eliminates their weaknesses when properly constituted and maintained. Other writers who came along much later did suggest similar ideas, such as Quality Circles, but few if any of them envisioned applying their notions as widely as Dr. Hill did. The Master Mind can be used in almost any situation. Dr. Hill did not imagine it as something limited to the workplace, but a tool that could be created whenever and wherever the need arose.

The basis for the Master Mind is something Dr. Hill

called "mental chemistry." Just as physical science has advanced over the decades, our understanding of human thinking has changed as well. Dr. Hill was thinking on the cutting edge when he wrote *The Ladder to Success*. He understood the *essence* of the way that minds interact, although his speculation about some of the mechanics has been disproved. Still, he put his finger on significant ideas that you can learn to apply.

The chapter begins, however, by addressing something more basic to the pursuit of success: desire.

THE TEXT
The Starting Point of Success

Just as the oak tree... sleeps within the acorn, *success* begins in the form of an intense *desire*. Out of strong desires grow the motivating forces which cause men to cherish hopes, build plans, develop courage, and stimulate their minds to a highly intensified degree of action in pursuit of some *definite* plan or purpose.

Desire, then, is the starting point of all human achievement. There is nothing back of desire except the stimuli through which *strong desire* is fanned into a hot flame of *action.* These stimuli are known and have been included as a part of the Law of Success philosophy described in this book.

It has been said, and not without reason, that one may have anything one wants, within reasonable limitations, providing *one wants it badly enough!* Anyone who is capable of stimulating the mind to an intense state of *desire* is capable also of more than average achievement in the pursuit of that desire. It must be remembered that *wishing* for a thing is not the same as *desiring* it with such intensity that out of this desire grow impelling forces of action which drive one to build plans and put those plans to work. A wish is merely a passive form of desire. Most people never advance beyond the wishing stage.

Why, you may be asking, is this discussion preceding a chapter on the Master Mind? It's true that in later works, Dr. Hill began with the lesson on a Definite Purpose—dedicating yourself to a clearly defined goal—which seems to tie more neatly to the topic of desire. But here, in *The Ladder of Success*, Dr. Hill is aiming toward a discussion of the mental state of the Master Mind participants and what seems to be a digression will fit neatly with what follows.

Because the Master Mind is such a distinctive part of his philosophy, Dr. Hill began his first two books by addressing it. It is an unusual idea and he was understandably interested in setting his work apart from other authors. In later works, it is the second principle discussed, most likely because the author realized that the issues of desire and purpose were so fundamental to the pursuit of success that nothing else could be treated as practically until they had been covered. Here, he simply solves that problem in a different way, by discussing the motivation for success in another context, but his comments are still important. We'll look at them briefly and return to them in discussing the second chapter.

The text emphasizes the difference between a wish and a desire. Wishes produce nothing, but desire is transforming, changing first a person and then the world. The proof of the existence of desire is action in pursuit of one's desire. Proper mental activity results in physical activity. Action is stressed in the beginning and throughout the book.

Moving from wishing to desiring is an enormous stumbling block to most people. They have ideas of what they want from life, but are never able to fan the embers of their wishes into a burning desire. If they find themselves by luck in a good situation, they continue on as before, doing nothing to improve their lot; if they find themselves in a bad situation, they curse their luck, but never manage to alter their circumstances.

People with a burning desire, on the other hand, become dynamos, engines of mental and physical activity that begin altering the landscape around them, smoothing over bumps, and laying down roads that take them where they want to be. These are the people who are headed for success. They represent the expression of an aphorism that Dr. Hill made justifiably famous:

"Whatever the mind can conceive and believe, it can achieve."

Is there something that burns inside you? It needs to be more than a vague dissatisfaction with your current situation, no matter how unattractive you find life right now. And it cannot arise from something other people expect; you will not become successful because your family trusts it will happen. You need to find a spark of ambition, an idea that inflames your imagination and makes you want to act.

This burning desire, this passion, is what sets people like Steve Case or Kay Bailey Hutchison apart from the dreamers who think they might make good CEO's or United States Senators. It gets Steven Spielberg out of bed in the morning, and turns Mia Hamm into a star forward on the soccer field. They know what is important to them–from corporate policy and funding medical research, to filmmaking and scoring a goal.

So what? you think. *I know what I want. I am just not getting it. What do these people have that I don't? What is it that turns their wishes into desires?*

There are eight basic motivating forces, one or more of which is the starting point of all noteworthy human achievement. These motivating forces are:
1. The urge of self-preservation
2. The desire for sexual contact
3. The desire for financial gain
4. The desire for life after death
5. The desire for fame; to possess *power*
6. The urge of *love* (separate and distinct from sex urge)
7. The desire for revenge (prevalent in the more undeveloped minds)
8. The desire to indulge one's egotism.

Dr. Hill modified this list and expanded it in later writings. He added the desire for physical and mental freedom, and recognized that fame and egotism were better described as the desire for self-expression with all its positives and negatives. Revenge, he understood, was really the manifestation of two forces, anger and hate. And he included fear as a basic motive, a topic that will be addressed in more detail later. A more complete list, then, would look

like this one, taken from *Napoleon Hill's Keys to Success:*
1. self-preservation
2. love
3. fear
4. sex
5. desire for life after death
6. freedom for mind and body
7. anger
8. hate
9. desire for recognition and self-expression
10. wealth

Now, one could argue that there are other motives at work among people which are as varied as mischief and altruism, physical pleasure and curiosity. Yet all these other motives come back in the end to one of the fundamentals. Mischief arises from a mixture of self-expression and hate or anger, while altruism springs from love and often the desire for life after death. The desire for physical pleasure, as Dr. Freud would likely agree, is usually a sublimated desire for sexual pleasure. And curiosity, as wonderful and as valuable as it is, can spring from a mixture of fear and the urge for self-expression

The key point about these motives, whatever their number, is:

[People] make use of great power only when urged by one or more of these eight basic motives. The imaginative forces of the human mind become active only when spurred on by the stimulation of well-defined *motive!*

The question we hope you're asking yourself is:

what basic motive is driving me?

When you dream of success, what truly defines it for you? Is it cash or power? Prestige or admiration? Triumph over your enemies or freedom from want?

Answer honestly. There's no point in deceiving yourself about your basic motive. It's much better to realize what you want so that you can pursue it directly. Steven Spielberg is wealthy, yes, but wealth is a side-effect of pursuing his dream. Kay Bailey Hutchinson is powerful, but governmental power is only a tool she wields to affect policy in the hope of preserving American freedoms.

Dr. Hill does not spend any time moralizing about these different motives, though it is clear through occasional comments that he believed some are more worthy than others. All of them, however, have the power to make people successful.

This is a significant concept. Dr. Hill was a long way from blindly admiring every successful person he met, even giants like Andrew Carnegie and Henry Ford, who were undoubtedly paragons of success by nearly every standard. In his magazine, Hill blasted Carnegie for anti-competitive practices. He also saw that the single-mindedness which made Ford an automotive king would also later cripple his company as it turned to narrow vision and an unwillingness to change. But at this point, Dr. Hill is interested in the root of what made people successful and he has put his finger on it:

If you would achieve great success,
plant in your mind a strong motive!

People who find themselves stalled are often caught between several different motives. Most often, they want money or fame, but they also want security and familiarity. They won't make significant changes in their lives because they don't really want to give up some of the things they enjoy. Perhaps it's a secure but low-paying job. Free time, a lack of responsibility, the comfort of doing what they have always done–any of these acts as a brake on their desire for success.

What they need to do–perhaps what *you* need to do–is recognize your deepest ambition. If it's keeping everything on an even keel, you might just as well put this book down and not pick it up again. But if your ambition is something more, then you need to start concentrating on resisting the lure of the familiar. Turning a smoldering desire into a burning desire takes mental effort; the next chapter will show you ways to accomplish this.

And what of the darker motives, such as revenge, anger, and hate? Can you begin with one of these and look forward to the same prosperity as someone motivated by love or money?

Readers familiar with all Seventeen Principles will realize that these motives are very hard to reconcile with other ideas that are integral to Dr. Hill's philosophy. Even the Master Mind to which Dr. Hill is leading us in this lesson is likely to be hampered by motives such as hate.

But it's not impossible to achieve a certain kind of greatness when motivated by the darker side of human nature. In *The Law of Success*, Hill presented a table in which he ranked historical figures according to their adherence to his Principles. Abraham Lincoln, Benjamin Franklin, and George Washington all got high scores, but Hill included two famous examples of men who had won accolades but ultimately saw their dreams dashed because they could not adhere to all the necessary elements of a truly successful life. They were Napoleon Bonaparte, one-time ruler of most of Europe who died in exile on a lonely South Atlantic Island, and Jesse James, the train robber. (In what must have been a mild swipe at then-President Calvin Coolidge, Hill ranked him one point below Bonaparte but still called him a success.)

It's easy to think of other people who won great fame (or infamy) in the pursuit of their goals only to see their final ambitions dashed by the forces they essentially unleashed against themselves. Sometimes we call this tragedy and sometimes we call this justice. It's also true that evil and despicable people don't always come to ruin. For every Adolf Hitler there is a Josef Stalin, a monster who goes to his grave unrewarded for the evil he has done.

Does this mean that you don't need to worry about your basic motive? Not a bit. To begin, you need to know what drives you simply because not knowing will mean that you can never begin to satisfy yourself. What does money mean to someone who hungers for love? What pleasure is there in sex when hatred is what drives you? No matter how much you attain in life, none of it will mean anything if it doesn't fulfill that burning desire inside you.

And what if you are driven by something like anger or hatred? Does admitting that free you to pursue your desire no matter the consequences? At this point, Dr. Hill is only hinting, but later the answer will clearly be no. What then, are you supposed to do with the compelling if unsavory urge that drives you?

Dark motives have shocked many people out of lives of lethargy. Noble motivations have caused misery and suffering around the world. It's far better that you have a dark motive and full awareness than noble desire and fuzzy awareness.

But beginning with a motive you don't like to acknowledge doesn't mean that you'll spend the rest of your life pursuing it, at least not when you learn and apply Dr. Hill's other ideas. Dark desires have a way of giving way to the satisfactions brought by living according to the Seventeen Principles. The sense of your own potential that you gain will, in a very real way, enlighten you. If you start out in pursuit of piles of money you won't necessarily end up in the Peace Corps, but your ideas of what to do with your gains will expand and you'll find that you won't be satisfied with a hefty bank account alone. You'll want more. Desire, as we have already seen, is a transforming force.

In short, it's better to admit your motivation and its shortcomings and act accordingly than to wait around for a loftier notion to strike. It may never come to you as long as all you can think about is the desire you are not fulfilling.

In a strikingly forthright manner, Dr. Hill points out the value and importance of discovering your motive:

> Power and success are synonymous terms. Success is not attained through honesty alone, as some would have us believe. The poorhouses are filled with people who, perhaps, were honest enough. They failed to accumulate money because they lacked the knowledge of how to acquire and use *power*!

So just what is power and how can you get it?

Physical Power

There are two forms of power which we shall analyze in this lesson. One is mental power, and it is acquired through the process of thought. It is expressed through definite plans of action, as the result of organized knowledge. The ability to think, plan, and act through a well-organized procedure is the starting point of all mental power.

The other form of power is physical. It is expressed through natural laws, in the form of electrical energy, gravitation, steam pressure, etc. In this lesson we shall analyze both mental and physical power and explain the relationship between these two.

Knowledge, alone, is not power. *Great personal power* is acquired only through the harmonious cooperation of a number of people who concentrate their efforts upon some definite plan.

You might expect that Dr. Hill would at this point dive into a discussion of mental power, since it is the heart of the subject. Our mental powers are unique to each of us and thus the foundation for our potential successes. Instead, he first discusses physical power. Why? Because he plans to challenge our ideas about mental power with some surprising ideas of his own, and he wants us to see that these ideas have a basis in science and are not simply mumbo-jumbo.

Dr. Hill embarks on a discussion of atomic structure, marveling that matter is composed entirely of energy that behaves according to fixed principles:

In the world of physical matter, whether one is looking at the largest star that floats through the heavens or the smallest grain of sand to be found on earth, the object under observation is but an organized collection of molecules, atoms, and electrons[1], revolving at inconceivable speed.

Every particle of physical matter is in a continuous state of highly agitated motion. Nothing is ever still, although nearly all physical matter may appear, to the physical eye, to be motionless...

We are rarely conscious of this "continuous state of highly agitated motion," but it is the basis for all chemical and most physical processes, as the energies of atoms and molecules attract and repel each other, combining to form new substances or producing reactions such as combustion.

Another effect of motion is vibration. Dr. Hill points out that we can detect certain kinds of vibrations with our five normal senses: sound, heat, and light are all examples, in increasing intensity.

And still higher up the scale, just how high no one at present seems to know, vibrations create the power with which man *thinks*.

---

[1] We now know that atomic structure is more complex than this description, but the essential point that all matter is composed of particles of energy in constant motion remains valid

Now, we are closing in on the crucial point, for if sound, heat and light are all transmitted outward from their sources, may not thoughts be also?

Science identified brain waves as a form of energy–just like light–many years ago. Alpha waves, which are generated in states of mental relaxation, have an intensity of 8-13 hertz, much less than Dr. Hill speculated. Beta waves, which occur during states of full alertness, are in the range of 13-30 hertz. Does the fact that he missed his guess about the frequency matter? No. What is significant is that the energy is produced by the activity of our brains.

Dr. Hill then turns to one of the most influential scientific figures of the previous century to make his keenest point. Dr. Alexander Graham Bell invented the telephone, a device which transmits sound by converting the vibrations of sound waves into an electrical current and then reconverts the current into sound waves at another location. Bell himself was vastly intrigued by the idea that energy could be transferred from one place to the next and carry with it its original characteristics. Advances in what he called "wireless" transmission, which we have come to know most commonly in radio and television, only further stimulated Dr. Bell's thinking. (Think how excited he would be by the internet, cell phones and MRIs!) The inventor notes:

'We may indulge in some speculations based on what we know of the wireless waves, which, as I have said, are all we can recognize of a vast series of vibrations which must exist. If the thought waves are similar to the wireless waves, they must pass from the brain and flow endlessly around the world and the universe. The body and the skull and other solid obsta-

21

cles would offer no obstruction to their passage, as they pass through the ether which surrounds the molecules of every substance, no matter how solid and dense.

'You ask if there would not be constant interference and confusion if other people's thoughts were flowing through our brains and setting up thoughts in them that did not originate with ourselves?

'How do you know that other men's thoughts are not interfering with yours now? I have noticed a good many phenomena of mind disturbances that I have never been able to explain. For instance, there is the inspiration or the discouragement that a speaker feels in addressing the audience. I have experienced this many times in my life and have never been able to define exactly the physical causes of it....

'Briefly, the hypothesis that mind can communicate directly with mind rests on the theory that thought or vital force is a form of electrical disturbance that can be taken up by induction and transmitted to a distance ...'

Relentless science fictions, outright frauds, and entertainers who earn a living by illusion have all given the idea of mental communication a shabby name. Neither Dr. Hill nor Dr. Bell imagined bending spoons, walking on hot coals, or cheating at cards as the significant import of the idea of mental connections between people. And Dr. Hill certainly did not find the subject intriguing because it would allow for mental telepathy along the lines of that seen in movie plots.

What he was striving to underscore is the notion that your mental energy has a role to play outside the operation of your brain. First, by leading you to action, it alters the outside world. That impact is undeniable. But what he also wants you to consider is the potential your mind has for both sending out and receiving energy. And the likeliest place for this energy to have an effect is not on the spoon that a psychic bends, but on other minds which are operating on the basis of the same energies.

Dr. Hill described these effects as the result of "mental chemistry." This seems to be a somewhat inaccurate term, since physics appears to play a greater role than chemistry in the contact between minds. But it is true that most brain activity is the result of chemical interactions between cells. Endorphins, for example, are chemicals emitted by certain brain cells that create the sensation of pleasure. Memory appears to operate through chemical reactions between cells dedicated to this purpose. Even the electricity that produces brain waves is generated by chemical processes.

Mental chemistry, then, would seem worth investigating.

The Chemistry of the Mind

Dr. Hill returns to discussing the reactions people have upon meeting each other:

> Some minds are so naturally adapted to each other that 'love at first sight' is the inevitable outcome of the contact. Who has

not known of such an experience? In other cases, minds are so antagonistic that violent mutual dislike shows itself at the first meeting. These results occur without a word being spoken, and without the slightest signs of any of the usual causes for love and hate acting as a stimulus.... The effects of the meeting of the two minds is obvious to even the most casual observer. Every effect must have a cause! What could be more reasonable than to suspect that the cause of the change in mental attitude between the two minds, which have just come into contact, is none other than the disturbance of the electrons or units of each mind in the process of rearranging themselves in the new field created by the contact.

Stated another way, the mental attitude of one person affects the mental attitude of people nearby. A mind obsessed with fear will begin to instill fear in others. A greedy mind, a happy mind, a peaceful mind, all will have an effect on other minds they contact. And of course, minds that are charged with a different kind of energy will sense this and adapt. The nature of this adaptation is the source of emotional responses to new people; some will seem to be close kin, while others will be so different in orientation that we are angered or frightened by their energy or mental chemistry.

Dr. Hill provides numerous examples of the short-term and long-term effects of mental chemistry between people. Marriages and romantic relationships, he notes, may be forged on the basis of an initially favorable reaction, but

The entire civilized world knows that the first two or three years of association after marriage are often marked by much disagreement of a more or less petty nature. These are the years of "adjustment"...

While there are other contributing causes, the main lack of harmony during these early years of marriage is due to the slowness of the chemistry of the minds blending harmoniously. Stated differently, the electrons or units of energy called the mind are often neither extremely friendly nor antagonistic on first contact, but through constant association they gradually adapt themselves in harmony, except in rare cases where association has the opposite effect of leading eventually to open hostility between these units...

So marked is the effect of the chemistry of the human minds that any experienced public speaker may quickly interpret the manner in which his statements are accepted by the audience. Antagonism in the mind of but one person in an audience of one thousand may be readily detected by the speaker who has learned how to "feel" and register the effects of antagonism. Moreover, the public speaker can make these interpretations without observing or in any manner being influenced by the expression on the faces of those in his audience. On account of this fact, an audience may cause a speaker to rise to great heights of oratory, or heckle him into failure, without making a sound or denoting a single expression of satisfaction or dissatisfaction through the features of the face.

All "Master Salesmen" know the moment the "psychological time for closing" has arrived, not by what the prospective buyer says, but from the effect of the chemistry of his mind as interpreted or "felt" by the salesman. Words often belie the intentions of those speaking them, but a correct interpretation of the chemistry of the mind leaves no loophole for such a possibility. Every able salesman knows that the majority of buyers have a habit of affecting a negative attitude almost to the very climax of the sale.

...Every mind has what might be termed an electrical field. The nature of this field varies, depending on upon the "mood" of the individual mind back of it, and upon the nature of the chemistry of the mind creating the "field"...

It is believed by this author that the normal and or natural condition of the chemistry of any individual mind is the result of his physical heredity, plus the nature of the thoughts which have dominated that mind; that every mind is continuously changing to the extent that the individual's philosophy and general habits of thought change the chemistry of his or her mind.... That the individual may voluntarily change his mind so that it will either attract or repel all with whom it comes in contact is a *known fact!* Stated in another manner, any person may assume a mental attitude which will attract and please others or repel and antagonize them, and this without the aid of words or facial expression, or other form of bodily movement or demeanor.

If you're already familiar with Dr. Hill's work, you're likely to be nodding now. The idea of a Positive Mental Attitude is a cornerstone of much of his later writing and an invaluable tool. PMA brings many more advantages than its effect on the people you meet, but anyone who has worked at developing a positive state of mind knows that you do become a catalyst for change in the attitudes of other people. And the same, unfortunately, is true when you embrace a negative state of mind. You bring out negativity in others, often directed at yourself. It's simple mental chemistry.

These mental interactions take place all the time, whether we recognize them or not. Depending on our own attitudes, they are helpful or harmful, so it would seem very advantageous to embrace PMA and put a positive spin on all the connections we make, from the most intimate to the most casual.

Mind Chemistry and Economic Power

But what if there were a way to create the connection regularly, using a clearly defined focus, and with a purpose in mind? This connection is exactly what a Master Mind achieves.

27

A Master Mind may be created through the bringing together of blending, in a spirit of perfect harmony, of two or more minds. Out of this harmonious blending, the chemistry of the mind creates a third mind which may be appropriated and used by one or all of the individual minds. This Master Mind will remain available as long as the friendly, harmonious alliance between the individual minds exists. It will disintegrate and all evidence of its existence disappear the moment the friendly alliance is broken.

The essential harmony between participants in a Master Mind can be created in a number of ways:
Every sales manager and every military commander and every leader in any other walk of life understand the necessity of an "esprit de corps"–a spirit of common understanding and co-operation–in the attainment of success. This mass spirit of harmony of purpose is attained through discipline, voluntary or forced, of such a nature that the individual minds become blended into a "Master Mind," by which is meant that the chemistry of these individual minds is modified in such a manner that these minds blend and function as one. The methods through which this "blending" process takes place are as numerous as are the individuals engaged in the various forms of leadership. Every leader has his or her own method of co-ordinating the minds

of the followers. One will play on the fear of
penalties, while another plays upon rewards, in
order to reduce the individual minds of given
groups of people to where they may be blended into a mass mind. The student will not
have to search deeply into history of statesmanship, politics, business, or finance, to discover the technique employed by the leaders
in these fields in the process of blending the
minds of individuals into a mass mind.

In other words, leaders create Master Minds by
being fully aware of the basic human motives which Dr. Hill
has already discussed. Dr. Hill is speaking here in general
terms, and his use of the phrase "mass mind," should not
lead you to assume that you require an army or vast numbers
of followers to create a Master Mind. Remember, it takes
only two minds to begin reaping the benefits of a Master
Mind. In fact, Dr. Hill suggests that six or seven people may
be the most effective number for a Master Mind, but having
more or fewer participants should not discourage you from
starting such a group. You need only two people for a Master
Mind to be created.

Yet, what are the benefits to be gained from a Master
Mind? Most potently:

When two or more people harmonize
their minds and produce the effect known as a
"Master Mind," each person in the group
becomes vested with the power to contact with
and gather knowledge through the subconscious" minds of all the other members of the
group. This power becomes immediately

noticeable, having the effect of stimulating the mind to a higher rate of vibration and otherwise evidencing itself in the form of a more vivid imagination and the consciousness of what appears to be a sixth sense. It is through this sixth sense that new ideas will "flash" into the mind. These ideas take on the nature and the form of the subject dominating the mind of the individual. If the entire group has met for the purpose of discussing a given subject, ideas concerning that subject will come pouring into the minds of all present, as if an outside force were directing them. The minds of those participating in the "Master Mind" become as magnets, attracting ideas and thought stimuli of the most highly organized and practical nature...

The process of mind blending here described as a "Master Mind" may be likened to the act of one who connects many electric batteries to a single transmission wire, thereby stepping up the power passing over that line by the amount of energy the batteries carry. Just so in the case of blending individual minds into a "Master Mind." Each mind, though the principle of mind chemistry, stimulates all the other minds of the group, until the mind energy this becomes so great that it penetrates and connects with the universal energy

An amazing assertion, no doubt, and one which is enormously significant to anyone hoping to achieve something in life. Stated a little less emphatically, Dr. Hill's idea is that a group of minds focused on a single goal has the ability to amplify the work that each mind does.

The advantages are boundless inspiration, enhanced creativity, resolved problems, abundant enthusiasm, and efficient work.

Why don't more people reap them?

Conflicting ambitions usually prevent a Master Mind from operating. Consider two young men working out of a garage who were able to pool their knowledge and vision in a Master Mind to create Apple Computers, a company which launched the personal computer revolution, and rattled the likes of IBM. Steve Jobs and Steve Wozniak did not have the financial resources or engineering expertise available to big corporations, but they created success by concentrating all their mental faculties on a single goal.

Eventually, Apple became a big company, but like IBM and other behemoths, it stumbled. Instead of focusing all the energy of two employees on a single mission, the company had multiple missions, such as satisfying corporate clients, attracting new home users, developing new operating systems, and pleasing stockholders. The Master Mind ceased to exist and Apple lost the edge that it once had.

Big organizations have their own advantages, but it is exceedingly rare for top executives to unite everyone behind a single mission and create a Master Mind that includes all employees. There is too much competition for resources, too much jockeying for personal advancement over company advantage. The salespeople want lower prices, the stockholders want a stronger bottom line, the public relations team suggests inventive new promotion schemes and the legal department is worried about liability issues.

Contrast this, then, with a small group. Each participant knows what their purpose is in working together. Each can see the costs and benefits of a course of action. They brainstorm freely, think aloud with each other, and imagine that if any one of them succeeds, the others succeed, as well. That is the kind of close-knit functioning that comes from a Master Mind. That is the power of a Master Mind.

Dr. Hill discusses a Master Mind that he saw at work in his day, between three important public figures. They did not call it a Master Mind, but that is what they had created. They were Henry Ford, Thomas Edison, and Harvey Firestone, founder of the tire company that bears his name. The three were friends, and for many years vacationed together. Dr. Hill found it remarkable that all three, who had little in the way of formal education and came from ordinary backgrounds and families of little wealth, had achieved such great heights in their lives. The bond between them, he speculated, allowed them to knock ideas around, keep abreast of new information, and recognize opportunities for applying new ideas, which they created in abundance.

(In light of this, it seems somewhat sadly ironic to reflect on the rift between the Ford Motor Company and Firestone Tires many years later. The dispute over responsibility surrounding problems with tires for the Ford Explorer might have taken a very different path if Henry Ford and Harvey Firestone had been able to sit down together and talk it over. Both companies might have helped rather than hurt their reputations, and lives might have been saved.)

Dr. Hill saw a similar connection between a group of Chicago businessmen known as the Big Six, and among executives at what was then known as the United States Steel Corporation. These same mental bonds are at work in successful endeavors all over the world today. Steven Spielberg works with Jeffrey Katzenberg and David Geffen at Dreamworks Pictures, and if Spielberg's name appears more often in the papers, that hardly means the other two are not contributing in a profound way to their company's success. Dreamworks is a large company, but even if a Master Mind does not encompass everyone who works there, it's reasonable to assume that part of its success arises from the working relationship between the men who run it.

As Dr. Hill points out:

Search where you will and wherever you find an outstanding success in business, finance, or industry, or in any of the professions, you may be sure that back of the success is some individual who has applied the principle of mind chemistry through which a "Master Mind" has been created. These outstanding successes appear to be the handiwork of but one person, but search closely and the other individuals whose minds have been co-ordinated with his own may be found.

Power (man power) *is organized knowledge, expressed through intelligent action!*

No effort can be said to be *organized* unless the individuals engaged in the effort co-ordinate their knowledge and energy in a spirit of perfect harmony. Lack of such harmonious co-ordination of effort in the main cause of practically every business failure.

Dr. Hill then relates a story from a class he had taught. He asked his students to write an essay describing Henry Ford's wealth. Most of them produced descriptions of cash and stock, plants and inventory, but one asserted:

'Henry Ford's assets consist, in the main, of two items, viz: (1) Working capital and raw and finished materials; (2) The knowledge, gained from experience, by Henry Ford himself, and the co-operation of a well-trained organization which understands how to apply this knowledge to best advantage from the Ford viewpoint. It is impossible to estimate, with anything approximating correctness, the actual dollars and cents value of either of these two groups of assets, but it is my opinion that their relative values are:

The organized knowledge of the Ford Organization 75%.

The value of cash and physical assets of every nature, including raw and finished materials 25%.

This is an idea with which Dr. Hill emphatically agrees. He notes:

Unquestionably the biggest asset that Henry Ford has is his own brain. Next to this would come the brains of his immediate circle of associates, for it has been through co-ordination of these that the physical assets which he controls were accumulated.

Destroy every plant the Ford Motor Company owns; every piece of machinery; every ton of raw or finished material; every finished automobile, and every dollar on deposit in any bank, and Ford would still be the most powerful man, economically, on earth. The brains which have built the Ford business could duplicate it again in short order. Capital is always available in unlimited quantities, to such brains as Ford's.

Economically, Ford is the most powerful man on earth, because he has the keenest and most practical conception of *organized knowledge* of any man on earth, as far as this author has the means of knowing.

Henry Ford, of course, did not remain the most economically powerful person on earth. Dr. Hill goes on to mention what he calls some "blunders" on Ford's part, though he is not specific about what they are. The seeds of trouble were there in Ford's famous pronouncement that his customers could have any color car they wanted, as long as it was black. It's worth noting, though, that Ford was surpassed by General Motors in the two decades that followed the publication of *The Ladder of Success*. One quality that is often cited to explain GM's rise at Ford's expense is the upstart company's willingness to seek new ideas from talented design teams at a time when Ford cars showed little innovation. Though Henry Ford may have become the earliest automotive titan, the Master Mind, it seems, was employed at GM.

It would be difficult today to single out the world's most economically powerful person. But if Steve Case or Bill Gates were suddenly unemployed, is there any doubt that people with the proven ability to build successful companies would have trouble starting over again and thriving? Yes, there are always situations where someone gets a lucky break, but lucky breaks don't last. They have to be built upon.

The ability to build on whatever assets you have is what Dr. Hill calls "organized knowledge." Organized knowledge translates to power, we have seen, and

Power and success are synonymous terms! One grows out of the other; therefore, any person who has the knowledge and ability to develop power, through the principle of harmonious co-ordination of effort between individual minds, or in any other manner, may be successful in any reasonable undertaking that is possible of successful termination.

Obviously, the more knowledge you are able to muster and make use of, the better off you are. Organized knowledge is worth more than capital or prestige because it can be transformed into those assets. Through the Master Mind, you amplify both your knowledge and your ability to apply it effectively. What, then, does it take to make a Master Mind work?

The Psychology of Harmony

Dr. Hill begins his next section with a caution:

It must not be presumed that a "Master

Mind" will immediately spring, mushroom fashion, out of every group of minds which make a pretense of co-ordination in a spirit of *harmony.*

Harmony, in the real sense of the word, is as rare among groups of people as is genuine Christianity among those who proclaim themselves Christians.

Harmony is the nucleus around which the state of mind known as the "Master Mind" must be developed. Without this element there can be no "Master Mind," a truth which cannot be repeated too often.

Woodrow Wilson had in mind the development of a "Master Mind," to be composed of minds representing the civilized nations of the world, in his proposal of the League of Nations. Wilson's conception was the most far-reaching humanitarian idea ever created in the mind of man, because it dealt with a principle which embraces sufficient power to establish a real Brotherhood of Man on earth. The League of Nations, or some similar blending of international minds, in a spirit of harmony, is sure to become a reality.

Dr. Hill was not alone in mourning the League of Nations, nor in predicting that it would have a successor: the United Nations. He was also enough of a patriot to gloss over the fact that a major factor in the failure of the League was the lack of participation by the United States, even though our own president had proposed it. The League floundered because its purpose required coordination among all the major world powers: without the United States, it simply did not have the harmony it needed to carry out its mission. It was a might-have-been Master Mind.[2]

Harmony, of course, is elusive. Dr. Hill cites the example of old-fashioned religious revival meetings (even in 1930, he saw them as "old"). The mental energy of a revival meeting is powerful, but fleeting. The same is true of a sales seminar, or an organizational retreat, when participants gather, brainstorm, create bonds and enjoy comradery.

Call it psychology, mind chemistry, or anything you please (they are all based on the same principle), but there is nothing more certain than the fact that whenever a group of minds are brought into contact in a spirit of *perfect harmony,* each mind in the group becomes immediately supplemented and re-enforced by a noticeable energy called a "Master Mind"....

It is no wonder that leaders in business and industrial enterprises, as well as those in other fields of endeavor, find it so difficult to organize groups of people so they will function without friction in the attainment of a given objective. Each individual human being possesses forces, within himself, which are difficult to harmonize, even when he is placed in

---

[2] The United Nations is not always an effective example of a Master Mind, either, though it does sometimes manage to rally itself when faced with significant crises. Though it stumbles often, it is worth remembering that the U.N. coordinated the effort to rid the world of smallpox, a devastating disease that had been a scourge throughout history. Such is the power of a Master Mind.

the environment most favorable to harmony. If the chemistry of the individual's mind is such that the units of his mind cannot be easily harmonized, think how much more difficulty it must be to harmonize a group of minds so that they will function as one, in an orderly manner, through what is known as a "Master Mind."

The leader who successfully develops and directs the energies of a "Master Mind" must possess tact, patience, persistence, self-confidence, intimate knowledge of mind chemistry, and the ability to adapt himself (in a state of perfect poise and harmony) to quickly changing circumstances without showing the least sign of annoyance.

One of the greatest benefits of the Principles of Success is the way in which it harmonizes the forces of your mind. Directed toward the fulfillment of a definite chief aim, your mind begins to avoid distractions. Lessons on self-confidence, imagination, enthusiasm, self-control, pleasing personality, accurate thinking, and concentration will all show you how to harmonize the forces within yourself so that you can become a more effective harmonizer of the forces in others.

The successful leader must posses the ability to change the color of his mind, Chameleon-like, to fit every circumstance that arises in connection with the object of his leadership. Moreover, he must possess the ability to change from one mood to another without showing the slightest signs of anger or lack of

self-control...
Without this ability no leader can be powerful, and without power no leader can long endure.

Creating harmony is a balancing act, and especially in a young Master Mind, it requires great effort. Yet it is worth noting that a little progress is quickly amplified; people enjoy being in harmony, especially productive harmony. Guide your Master Mind to its first achievement and its members will have ample cause to cooperate with your efforts to unify them. This is not to say that there will be no further signs of trouble, but just as any naval commander would rather sail into battle with a crew that has worked together, you will find that knowing the members of your Master Mind will allow you to lead them better.

The world cries out for leaders who can create harmony. Only the most desperate or despicable people fear it. Yet its creation is as much an art as a science, and you must not despair as you learn the ins and outs of inspiring harmony. Persistence and belief in your purpose will be your best supports in this effort, yet in every lesson that follows this one you will glean new ideas about ways that you can create the harmony you need.

This first lesson has been a long one. Dr. Hill has used it to introduce both his main themes: the power of the mind, and the importance of harmony. Now he will begin to move forward more briskly-energized, as it were, by the ideas he has laid out in Lesson One.

As you read what he has written, and consider the accompanying text, keep these two main ideas in your mind. The power of your mind and the power of harmony are essential for creating anything at all worthwhile, and you will see, lesson-by-lesson, how they can be directed for your own purposes. But make the effort to go beyond what is provided for you here and to discover applications of these ideas that are aligned with your own life and situation.

The Principles of Success are not a formula. They do not provide a series of seventeen easy steps to fame and fortune. They require your active involvement and full understanding before they will yield their greatest rewards. It is not simply a fringe benefit that they apply to every possible situation: they *must be applied* in every situation and adapted to those situations as only you can understand how.

These are Napoleon Hill's Principles of Success. The time has come to make them your Principles of Success.

Lesson Two
A DEFINITE CHIEF AIM

SUMMARY
Following his long and multifaceted discussion of the Master Mind and its implications, Napoleon Hill launches a series of succinct lessons that cover the principles of success as he then defined them. His opening statement in this chapter makes his point quite clearly:

To be successful in any sort of endeavor, you must have a *definite* goal toward which to work. You must have definite plans for attaining this goal. Nothing is ever accomplished that is worthwhile without a definite plan of procedure that is systematically and continuously followed day by day.

Hill gave the idea of the Definite Chief Aim great prominence in his writing because he understood that its absence was the single greatest barrier to human fulfillment. While the reasons why a person might not have a Definite Chief Aim are myriad, the result of its absence is predictable: failure.

Hill had come to this conclusion as the result of his many years spent interviewing the successful leaders of his day. As he would state over and over again during his lifetime, none of these men felt that they had reached their lofty positions by luck. While fortune is capable of providing extraordinary opportunity, it is just as likely to serve up disaster, and no one who achieves anything of lasting merit does so without first pursuing a purpose.

THE TEXT
Beating the Odds

During the past twenty years the author has analyzed more than twenty thousand people, in nearly all walks of life, and startling as it may seem, ninety-five per cent of those people were failures. By this is meant that they were barely making enough on which to exist, some of them not even doing this well. The other five per cent were successful, meaning by *"success"* that they were making enough for all their needs and laying something by for the sake of ultimate financial independence.

Now the significant thing about this discovery was that the five per cent who were succeeding had a *definite chief aim* and also a plan for attaining that aim. In other words, those who knew what they wanted, and had a plan for getting it, were succeeding while those who did not know what they wanted were *getting just that–nothing!*

This definition of success is somewhat tricky. "Ultimate financial independence" has to be defined individually. One person may envision a life of foreign travel, fine clothes and a well-stocked wine cellar; another may feel independence is reached without any of these luxuries and be quite content at a more modest level of living. In fact, if Dr. Hill were to evaluate your situation himself, his determination would not matter at all in comparison to your own assessment of your life.

Realizing that success is something you determine on your own is essential to formulating a definite chief aim. Will you never be satisfied without a Tuscan villa and your name in bold face type in the society columns? You will need a grander plan than someone for whom time with family and simple security are paramount.

This is not to say that you should settle for something less than your dream. Napoleon Hill's ideas will never lead you to sell yourself short. Success in many fields is not defined by financial progress. In science, the arts, community affairs, politics and the law, success comes through achievements that are often non-monetary and frequently tied to innovation, progress, or fame. The Principles of Success are just as useful for creating these rewards as they are for attaining financial independence.

Yet success, no matter how you define it, won't happen unless you construct both a personal definition and a plan for making it real. A definition—a concrete goal—is necessary on two levels. First, as we'll discuss at some length in a moment, it's impossible to plan without one. But keep this in mind: you cannot call yourself a success if you do not know how to define it.

This idea is so simple it's easy to overlook, but it often lies behind many people's sense of failure. Their definition of success is always fluid, always being shaped by what they see of other people's lives, what they read about in magazines, what they watch on television in advertisements and shows. In essence, they never become *someone else's idea of success* and regard themselves as failures. In the words of Charles Kingsley, they "act as though comfort and luxury were the chief requirements of life, when all that we need to make us really happy is something to be enthusiastic about."

Working out your own definition of success cuts away all the extraneous messages about what you need to do in order to call yourself a success. Maybe you do need eight percent body fat and a herd of polo ponies. Or maybe you need something else in order to feel that your life has been worthwhile. Perhaps what is most important to you is a reputation for skill in a job you love. If you're trying to figure out how to get those polo ponies, whatever it is that you truly value will get shifted to the back burner.

Napoleon Hill was not alone in recognizing the importance of setting down and sticking to a Definite Chief Aim. Though he was not the first writer to advocate a clear set of goals, he helped bring the idea into prominence in modern motivational literature. "In the long run," Henry David Thoreau wrote almost eighty years before, "men hit only what they aim at." Fifty years after Napoleon Hill began publishing, "goal setting" became a frequent topic of discussion. "Very few people are ambitious in terms of having a specific image of what they want to achieve," noted Judith Bardwick. "Most people's sights are only toward the next run, the next increment of money." And echoing Hill–though with a trifle more optimism—management guru Peter Drucker pointed out, "Management by objectives works if you know the objectives. Ninety percent of the time you don't."

You can set yourself apart from the do-nothing percent.

A Goal and a Plan Make all the Difference

In 1930, Napoleon Hill was writing to an audience in the grips of the Great Depression. Economic security was high on everyone's list of priorities as unemployment soared. Not surprisingly, Dr. Hill's examples were geared to addressing this pressing need. But a careful reader will see that he was not simply advocating getting rich as quickly as possible. He made a point of providing examples of people who could take justifiable pride in what they were doing. He noted:

If a man is engaged in the business of selling or rendering service which calls for methods of handling his customers that will cause them to patronize them continuously, he must have a *definite plan* for bringing about this result. The plan may be one thing, or it may be something else, but in the main it should be distinctive and of such a nature that it will impress itself on the minds of his patrons in a *favorable* manner. Anyone can hand out merchandise to those who come, voluntarily, and ask for it, but not everyone has acquired the art of delivering the merchandise that has that unseen "something" which causes the customer to repeat and come back for more. Here is where the necessity of a *definite chief aim* and definite plan for attaining it enters.

Within recent years, gasoline filling stations have become so numerous that one may be found just around the corner, so to speak, in every community. The gas, oil, and other supplies sold at the majority of these service stations is good, there being little difference between the quality received at one station and that received at another. Despite this fact, however, there are motorists who will drive miles out of their way, or delay the purchase of oil and gas until the very last minute, for the purpose of buying these supplies from some "favorite" service station.

Now the question arises, *"What causes these people to do this?"*

And the answer is, *"People trade at service stations where they are served by men who cultivate them."*

What is meant by *"men who cultivate them?"* It means that a few filling station men have created *definite plans* for studying and catering to motorists in such a manner that these motorists will return again. Good oil and gas, alone, cannot compete with the filling station manager who makes it his business to know people and cater to them according to their mannerisms and characteristics. One filling station manager makes it his business to watch the tires on every automobile that drives up, and when he sees a tire that needs more inflation, he promptly "gives it the air." If the windshield is dusty or dirty he wipes it with a wet cloth. If a car is covered with dust he gets busy with a duster. In these and scores of other ways, he impresses the motorist with the fact that he makes it his business to render service that is a bit different. All this does not "just happen." He has a *definite plan* and also a *definite purpose* in doing it, and that purpose is to bring motorists back to his station.

The world has changed since Napoleon Hill discoursed on gas stations, and some of the images he offers are almost quaint: imagine having your car dusted the next time you found a service station. But what Hill is doing with this story is impressing upon us, very clearly, the idea that success is not necessarily a matter of running a Fortune 500 corporation. More than seventy years ago, he saw success being created in places that were as humble then as they are now. And he admired that success and the vision that created it.

On your next stop for gas, ask yourself if you've arrived at a place where someone is trying to encourage you to return. You'll know it by a host of signs, from the way that the cashier (if there still is one) reacts to you, to the amenities that are offered along with the fill-up. Do you suppose that the gas station operates as it does by chance, or has someone made decisions–have they laid out a plan–for winning your repeat business? Good intentions are wonderful, but what counts for you as a customer is whether those intentions have been expressed carefully, in a way that makes a difference to your gas-buying experience.

It's through the careful expression of your own intentions that you demonstrate a clear goal and a precise plan for achieving it. If you've read other Napoleon Hill books, you know how important it is to make your definite chief aim concrete: you need to write it down. In a sentence or two, use positive and specific words to tell yourself what will make you a success in your own terms.

As soon as you've done this, immediately write down a plan for getting what you want. Set interim goals of things you need to accomplish next week, two months from now, next year and five years down the line. Make these goal statements highly specific, and attach dates to them so that you are providing yourself with a sense of urgency and–just as important–a sense of possibility. Your plan can be modified over time as you learn new things or see new opportunities, but you should always be aware of it, and always working to fulfill it. It should, in words Napoleon Hill used elsewhere, come to dominate your thoughts.

Here's why:

Let us now go a bit deeper into the study of the psychological principle upon which the law of a *definite chief aim* is based....The human mind is something like a magnet in that it will attract the counterpart of the dominating thoughts held in the mind, and especially those which constitute a definite chief aim or purpose. For example, if a man establishes as his definite chief aim, and as his daily working purpose, the adding of say one hundred new customers who will regularly purchase the merchandise or service he is rendering, immediately that aim or purpose becomes a dominating influence in his mind, and this influence will drive him to do that which is necessary to secure these additional one hundred customers.

Manufacturers of automobiles and other

lines of merchandise often establish what they call "quotas," covering the number of automobiles or the amount of merchandise that must be sold in each territory. These "quotas" when definitely established, constitute a definite chief aim toward which all who are engaged in the distribution of the automobiles or merchandise direct their efforts. Seldom does anyone fail to make the established quotas, but it is a well-known fact that had there been no "quotas" the actual sales would have been far less than they were with them. In other words, to achieve success in selling or in practically any other line of endeavor, one must set up a mark at which to shoot, so to speak, and without this target there will be but slim results.

One recent bestselling book enthusiastically endorses Dr. Hill's emphasis on the need for a goal and a plan. *Body for Life* by Bill Philips, a fitness program for exercise, diet and weight loss, heartily recommends the use of detailed, goal-oriented work-out routines. Philips urges his readers to enter their gyms with a minute-by-minute program for weight lifting, and as if Dr. Hill were whispering in his ear he writes, "If you fail to plan, you plan to fail."

During the Hundred Years War between England and France, a party of English soldiers led by Edward, the Black Prince, was overtaken near the town of Potiers by an army under the French king, Jean the Good. The English were outnumbered by two to one, and the French had brought what the chroniclers called the "flower" of the knighthood–all the greatest military men the country had.

Edward attempted a retreat, but was cut off, so he began for-tifying the ground he held and preparing for battle.

The French were eager to avenge the devastation the English had inflicted on the countryside, and all their lead-ers clamored to lead the assault. Three hundred of the most renowned knights led the charge. They were slaughtered.

Edward had arrayed his forces so that the only approach was through a narrow passage, too narrow for 300 horsemen. As the knight charged forward, English bowmen fired, not on the knights, but on their horses. The flight of arrows was so thick that "the sky was dark," and the heavi-ly armored knights were crushed under their horses; those who managed to roll clear were often unable to stand under the weight of the armor. King Jean's three top military offi-cials died in the onslaught.

Still the French kept coming and still the English fired. A second wave of French soldiers broke and fled back through the ranks of a third wave, which scattered in panic. As the desperate French tried to rally for a fourth assault, Prince Edward's archers rushed forward and reclaimed as many arrows as they could from among the fallen. They continued to pick off the French as they came onward and at last engaged the English directly. French numbers and valor finally seemed about to prevail.

But Prince Edward had planned even for this.

With a force of 400 fresh men he had held back, he charged into the midst of the French army. Panic ensued among common soldiers, and only around King Jean did any order remain. With his youngest son beside him, the King fought ferociously, but the fresh English warriors at last reached him. He surrendered.

The king of the greatest nation in Europe had been

captured by an army half the size of his. His best knights were slain, and all their prowess had come to naught. Humiliated, King Jean was packed off to England as a prisoner while the English celebrated in triumph.

King Jean had enjoyed all the obvious advantages that day: numbers, valor, and reputation were all on his side. But he entered into battle without a clear plan, falling back on what had always worked and not taking into account the English position or their powerful bowmen. Though Prince Edward was clearly not eager for battle, he triumphed by making sure that he would always exploit his strengths and undermine his opponent's weakness. A definite plan turned certain defeat into great success.

There are always distractions from the things you want to do. At home or at work, someone will need your help, demand your attention, or leave you a mess that requires cleaning up. These kinds of interruptions will always have the power to draw you off course–unless your mind is focused on your own goal and your own plans. It's not that you'll suddenly be freed from the need to attend to surprises, but you will find that 1) you can deal with them faster when your mind is attuned to your real purpose, and 2) that when you've put out these fires, you're better able to switch back into progress mode.

This ability to focus and stay on target is the result of a mind that is dominated by a definite chief aim. As Dr. Hill proclaims:

> The moment you write out a statement of your *chief aim*, your action plants an image of that aim firmly in your subconscious mind... [and] Nature causes your subconscious mind to use that *chief aim* as a pattern or blueprint

by which the major portion of your thoughts, ideas and efforts are directed toward the attainment of the objective on which the aim is based.

In short, create a goal and a plan, fix them in your mind, and you set yourself forth on the path.

Lesson Three
SELF-CONFIDENCE

SUMMARY
Belief in yourself and in all your abilities-chief among them your ability to succeed-is essential to implementing a plan of action. In this brief chapter, Napoleon Hill discusses the necessity of acting on the basis of belief. He also confronts fear, the chief cause of self-doubt, with the goal of helping you recognize the source of any lack of conviction in your ability to prosper.
Overcoming fear begins with recognizing it. Refusing to acknowledge fear and the resultant doubt only gives fear a greater power. There is no cowardice in admitting fear; bravery exists only when we act in spite of fear. And as we shall see, the key to acquiring the courage of Self-Confidence lies in your desire for success. As the great French novelist Marcel Proust noted, "Desire is indeed powerful; it engenders belief."

THE TEXT
An Active Faith
Napoleon Hill is characteristically direct in describing Self-Confidence, but he offers some important caveats that are worth exploring.

This term is self-explanatory–it means that to achieve success you must believe in yourself. However, this does not mean that you have no limitations; it means that you are to take an inventory of yourself, find out what qualities you have that are strong and useful, and then organize these qualities into a *definite plan of action* with which to obtain the object of your *definite chief aim...*

To succeed, you must have faith in your own ability to do whatever you make up your mind to do. Also, you must cultivate the habit of *faith* in those who are associated with you, whether they are in a position of authority over you, or you over them. The psychological reason for his will be covered thoroughly and plainly in the Law on *Co-operation* further on.

Doubters are not builders! Had Columbus lacked Self-Confidence and *faith* in his own judgment, the richest and most glorious spot of ground on this earth might never have been discovered, and these lines might never have been written. Had George Washington and his compatriots of the 1776 historical fame not possessed Self-Confidence, Cornwallis's armies would have conquered and the United States of America would be ruled today from a little island lying three thousand miles away in the East.

The word *faith* appears frequently in this chapter, which is not surprising given that Dr. Hill would later rename the principle of Self-Confidence as Applied Faith. He did not have specifically religious faith in mind, though that is certainly compatible with his point. Calling Self-

Confidence "Applied Faith" emphasized the dynamic nature of the proper attitude Dr. Hill wished to instill in his readers. He wanted to stress the necessity of an active pursuit of a plan, based upon an attitude of conviction.

In *The Ladder of Success,* he does so this way:

A definite chief aim is the starting point of all noteworthy achievement, but Self-Confidence is the unseen force which coaxes, drives, or leads on and on until the object of the aim is a reality. Without Self-Confidence man's achievements would never get beyond the "aim" stage, and mere aims, within themselves, are worth nothing. Many people have vague sorts of aims, but they get nowhere because they lack the Self-Confidence to create *definite plans* for attaining these aims.

Even more to the point, people without Self-Confidence lack the ability to act on their plans. They simply do not believe that acting will change anything about their lives. Action becomes, to them, worthless. If there's no point in acting, there is no point in taking risks or doing anything else to upset the status quo of their lives. Thus, through lack of Self-Confidence, they trap themselves in an endless cycle of demonstrating to themselves that nothing ever gets any better. In the words of Maxwell Maltz, "Of all the traps and pitfalls of life, self-disesteem is the deadliest and the hardest to overcome, for it is a pit designed and dug by our own hands, summed up in the phrase, 'It's no use, I can't do it.'"

One of Dr. Hill's favorite stories was of Thomas Edison and his countless trials to create a practical light bulb. Edison failed thousands of times in his efforts-a dismaying record-but he did not abandon his search. It would have been entirely human for him to throw up his hands and say, "It's no use, I can't do it," but he did not. He proceeded in his experiments; he acted as though success were possible, and so it became.

The Edison story is significant because it points out that success is not automatic with Self-Confidence. Edison did not succeed on the first try. You will likely fail at some things, too. But what Edison did do was continue to act in the belief that he could succeed, and this kind of action is at the core of what Dr. Hill would come to call Applied Faith.

Action-oriented Self-Confidence, or Applied Faith, is the willingness to accept risk and failure while believing that you are ultimately pursuing an attainable and worthy goal. And just as self-doubt engenders a self-perpetuating cycle, Applied Faith creates one as well. When you act with Self-Confidence, your chances of success increase, and with each success, you strengthen your Self-Confidence. Even failures can become sources of increased Self-Confidence, as Lesson 14 will discuss.

But Self-Confidence will never grow as long as it is held in check. Like a muscle, it needs exercise to stay toned, and with sufficient and regular use, it becomes stronger, more flexible, and acquires greater stamina. Give your Self-Confidence a workout plan like Bill Philips suggests in *Body for Life*: exercise it daily, and watch it grow strong.

You see here how a plan for your Definite Chief Aim dovetails nicely with building Self-Confidence.   You push yourself to do things you have not done before, and by doing so, you increase your ability to act Self-Confidently. With greater Self-Confidence, you are able to reach for higher goals and to make progress toward what you want in life.

Confronting Fear

Fear obviously has a hold on everyone at some point, or the world would be populated by people of utmost contentment, all of whom were achieving the maximum. It's human nature to experience fear. It's the nature of a successful person to confront and overcome fear. Dr. Hill tells us:

Fear is the main enemy of Self-Confidence. Every person comes into this world cursed, to some extent, with Six Basic Fears, all of which must be mastered before one may develop sufficient Self-Confidence to attain outstanding success.

These six basic fears are:
1. The Fear of Criticism
2. The Fear of Ill Health
3. The Fear of Poverty
4. The Fear of Old Age
5. The Fear of the Loss of Love of someone (ordinarily called jealousy)
6. The Fear of Death

Space will not permit a lengthy description of how and where these Six Fears come from. In the main, however, they were acquired through the early childhood environment by teaching, the telling of ghost stories, the discussion of "hell-fire," and in many other ways. Fear of Criticism is placed at the head of the list because it is, perhaps, the most common and one of the most destructive of the entire six fears.

Fear of Criticism is essentially a fear of failure, and the greatest enemy of Self-Confidence. What would you attempt today if you knew that no one would ever know that you failed? What do you never try because you are so certain that you will fail and be ridiculed for it? Do you keep your ideas to yourself at work? Do you never have a date because you cannot bear the thought of rejection? Do you stick with a line of work because you can't imagine what your friends and family would say if you told them what you really want to do? Fear of Criticism has you in its grasp.

How, then, do you overcome this fear? Recognizing that it is holding you back is the first step. Are there things that seem impossible for you to do? Why are they impossible? Is there some action that has no physical chance of success? Or are you afraid of being laughed at for falling on your face or trying something that others think just "isn't you"? If you can't bear the idea of telling someone else what you most want in life, you're being held back by Fear of Criticism.

Now ask yourself what it is you are truly putting at risk. Are you happy now? Will you be any more unhappy if you stick your neck out and venture something new? After all, you were discontented enough to envision a new way of life, to define it and to plan for it. It's human nature to want something better, and human nature to strive for it in the face of danger. "A ship in port is safe, " wrote Grace Murray Hopper, "but that's not what ships are built for."

You cannot wait around for success to find you. It won't. Success seeks people who seek it. It ignores people who only dream of it, who value it less than the comfort of the status quo. It cares much less about the assets you start with than the attitude you adopt in its pursuit. Failure, on the other hand, adores those who venture nothing, because it knows those people will never chase it away by summoning success to themselves.

Fear of Criticism is the most potent fear you will face in transforming your life. Begin your pursuit of success by confronting it, and you will gain the Self-Confidence to proceed through many other tasks.

Dr. Hill knew that the other Fears were less frequent causes of failure. Fear of Ill-Health tends to preoccupy people so that they can think of nothing else but the possibility of becoming sick. Fear of Poverty bind some folk so tightly to the idea of where tomorrow's dollars will come from that they cannot think a single day further into the future. The Fears of Old-Age and Death suggest that life has already passed by and there is no time left to make a difference. The Fear of the Loss of Love of Someone Else is jealousy, which so distorts a person's thinking that all resources are devoted to preventing the imagined loss. All these fears are paralyzing, just like the Fear of Criticism. In dealing with any of them, once you recognize what has you in its grips, you can rationally evaluate what is at stake and make a choice to defy and vanquish your fear.

The Great Antidote

Dr. Hill developed a concept after *The Ladder of Success*, most notably during his long association with W. Clement Stone, a man who embodied the ideals that Dr. Hill advocated. The idea of a Positive Mental Attitude distilled many aspects of the success principles that Dr. Hill taught. It is a powerful tool for dispelling fear, and of great use in applying all the other lessons in this book.

Positive Mental Attitude, often called simply PMA is, in Dr. Hill's words:

> a confident, honest, constructive state of mind which an individual creates and maintains by methods of his own choosing, through the operation of his own willpower, based on the motives of his own adaptation.

PMA is more than optimism or pragmatism, although both these qualities enter into it. It's a conviction that in any given circumstance, a favorable outcome is possible. It does not assume that a favorable outcome is automatic; PMA depends on a willingness and determination to work, and work hard, to create something worthwhile. In this respect, it requires faith in your own abilities. Fortunately, it also helps create that faith.

Recall the battle between the English and the French at Poitiers. The English faced a seemingly unwinnable situation. They could have surrendered on the spot, but instead, they looked for and created a situation in which they could triumph. Had they not acted as though they would win, they would have lost.

This is an example of how PMA builds Self-Confidence. When you envision a good result and can see how to achieve it, you gain the energy to pursue that result. You seize control of circumstances that might otherwise control you, and out of necessity, you set aside fear because you have given yourself a reason to do so. PMA does not always save you from defeat, but it does show you that there is always a way out. That lesson is well worth learning.

PMA does not require that you feel no fear; it simply allows you to act as if your fear is not the most powerful force in your life. In battling fear, perception is everything. When you come to understand that fear is controllable, you know in that moment how to control it: by acting as if it did not exist. In Shakespeare's words, "If you have not a virtue, assume it." To be courageous, act courageously.

As in any new activity that seems unfamiliar or strange to you, begin small if you doubt your ability to act. Just one or two occasions on which you surprise yourself by not enacting your fears will give you the courage to rise to greater challenges. If you wonder whether facing your fears is truly worth the trouble, consider the words of the great English essayist Sydney Smith:

> A great deal of talent is lost in the world for want of a little courage. Every day sends to their graves obscure men whom timidity prevented from making a first effort; who, if they could have been induced to begin, would in all probability have gone to great lengths in the career of fame. The fact is that to do anything in the world worth doing, we must not stand back shivering and thinking of the cold and danger, but jump in and scramble as well as we can.

Lesson Four
THE HABIT OF SAVING

SUMMARY

The Habit of Saving may seem an old-fashioned virtue in an age of derivative investments and leveraged buyouts, but Napoleon Hill saw more than the simple accumulation of a nest egg. Saving is not simply a matter of stuffing a mattress; it's a means to stockpiling opportunity and accumulating self-reliance.

We'll pay attention here to the idea of Habit, a force that works in everyone's life, though whether to positive or negative effect depends on the individual. Napoleon Hill placed enormous emphasis on the power of Habit in shaping a life, an idea that would later come to be recognized in other highly successful books. Gaining control of your habits is worthwhile in itself, and t he Habit of Saving is a worthy place to begin.

THE TEXT
Habitual Mastery

Never one to mince words, Napoleon Hill writes:

It is an embarrassing admission, but it is true, that a poverty-stricken person is less than the dust of the earth as far as the achievement of noteworthy success is concerned. It may be, and perhaps is true, that *money is not success*, but unless you have it or can command its use, you will not get far, no matter

63

what may be *your definite chief aim.*

This seems a harsh assessment. Is there no hope for someone starting out from rock bottom? Of course there is, according to the Habit of Saving. Dr. Hill is immediately at pains to make clear that money alone is not the point of his lesson:

> The amount saved from week to week or month to month is not of great consequence so long as the saving is regular and systematic. This is true because the *habit* of saving adds something to the other qualities essential for success which can be had in no other way.

That something is the understanding that you can create and direct your habits to your own benefit. In later writings, Dr. Hill would refer to "Cosmic Habitforce," a complex principle through which all the other principles of success reinforce each other, creating a whole that is greater than the sum of its parts. We'll address this idea more fully later, but for now keep in mind that control of your habits is extremely valuable.

As you may already be guessing, fear is a habit, a conditioned response to a certain stimulus that affects your behavior. Using PMA to face your fears weakens the Habit of Fear, which is why Self-Confidence is self-reinforcing. The Habit of Saving can also be self-reinforcing because you gain a reward each time you set a sum of money aside and see your bank balance increase:

> It is doubtful that any person can develop Self-Confidence to the highest possible point without the protection and independence

which belong to those who have saved and are saving money. There is something about the knowledge that one has some money ahead which gives faith and self-reliance such as can be had in no other way.

Why is this? Obviously, once you have saved money, even when you are confronted with the necessity of spending every dime, you have the knowledge that you can accumulate it again because you have the habit of doing so. If your savings are wiped out, instead of wallowing in despair, you will be able to get right back to work saving.

Each month that your bank balance increases–a defined, concrete measure of progress–you have tangible evidence of your ability to do something empowering and worthwhile. Your Fear of Failure is weakened by every deposit or transfer as you demonstrate to yourself that you've created a habit that always works to your benefit. You begin to understand just how powerful this ability is, and you wonder whether you can make it work in other ways.

Habits are stubborn. They are not created overnight, and they gain strength through repeated exercise, not grand gestures. You are better off setting aside ten dollars a week than ten thousand dollars tomorrow on impulse. "Habit is habit," wrote Mark Twain, "and not to be flung out the windows by any man but coaxed downstairs a step at a time." In forming any habit, begin with the possible and keep raising your sights rather than setting an outrageous goal. Repeated failure to create a new habit will, ironically, create another habit by itself: a habit of failure.

If any of the principles of success seem beyond your

present skills, keep in mind that you need to form none of them overnight. It's better that you raise them up on rock solid foundations than to proceed with shaky control of an ability you must depend on.

Stephen R. Covey, in his bestselling book *The 7 Habits of Highly-Effective People*, underscores the importance of getting a new habit off the ground well. He writes of the Apollo 11 voyage, when men first walked on the moon, and how inspiring it was:

> But to get there, those astronauts literally had to break out of the tremendous gravity pull of earth. More energy was spent in the first few minutes of lift-off, in the first few miles of travel, than was used over the next several days to travel half a million miles.

> Habits, too, have tremendous gravity pull—more than most people realize or would admit. Breaking deeply embedded habitual tendencies such as procrastination, impatience, criticalness, or selfishness that violate basic principles of human effectiveness involves more than a little willpower and a few minor changes in our lives. "Lift off" takes tremendous effort, but once we break out of the gravity pull, our freedom takes on a whole new dimension.

> Like any natural force, gravity pull can work with us or against us. The gravity pull of some of our habits may currently be keeping us from where we want to go. But it is also gravity pull that keeps our world together, that keeps the planets in their orbits and our universe in order. It is a powerful force, and if we use it effectively, we

can use the gravity pull of habit to create the cohesiveness and order to establish effectiveness in our lives.

Cash on Hand

The Habit of Saving brings more benefits than the Habit of Habit-forming, so to speak . Money in the bank is a powerful antidote to the Fear of Poverty, which loses its power to paralyze you when you know that you have prepared yourself to overcome it. It is also a source of independence, and not simply the sort associated with trust funds:

Without money, a person is at the mercy of every person who wished to exploit or prey upon him. If the man who does not save and has no money offers his personal services for sale he must accept what the purchaser offers; there is no alternative.

If opportunity to profit by trade or otherwise comes along, it is of no avail to the man who has neither the money or the credit, and it must be kept in mind that credit is generally based upon the money one has available or its equivalent.

For the sake of avoiding the term *financial independence*, and its association with retirement and achieved goals, let's think in terms of *financial liberty*: the freedom to make choices. The word liberty carries with it a connotation of possibility and self-determination, and it's easy to see how you might acquire financial liberty long before you are financially independent.

A comfortable amount of savings–and the sure knowledge that you know how to add to it and maintain it–brings freedom of choice in the pursuit of your goals. As Dr. Hill suggests, you gain the power to say "no," and "yes," in situations where before you had to obey the dictates of your wallet. There are countless ways you can exploit this liberty: freeing yourself from debt, taking a low-paying job that brings tremendous opportunity, or making an investment in the business you dream of owning.

Just what constitutes a "comfortable amount" is a question you will need to answer for yourself. Financial advisers such as Jane Bryant Quinn recommend a short-term savings fund of three months' living expenses. Retirement is another factor, and the sooner you begin saving for it, the better. But do not panic at the thought that you may now have nothing set aside or that you cannot begin an ambitious program tomorrow. Keep in mind always that regular and dependable savings may seem a slow way to start, but in adopting this approach you are also acquiring the power to control your habits.

Making a Habit of Saving will require some adjustments in your budgeting. Too many people are used to spending what they have on hand until it is gone, and then waiting for the next check. Then they spend again. You will have to become conscious of where your money goes, and when it goes out, and this is all to the good. You might just surprise yourself about how much cash seems to be spent on small things, and in moments when you think than an extra couple of dollars won't make any difference. But those extra dollars accumulate quickly.

Train yourself to watch your cash flow, and you'll

add a new aspect to your Habit of Saving: the Habit of Managing Money. You'll be on the lookout for the best uses of your money, not necessarily the easiest, and you will lead yourself to realize that the small sum you regularly set aside could be larger. Finding another fifty dollars to save each month is a much more satisfying activity than finding another fifty dollars to make a credit card payment.

Dr. Hill warns us:

> The Spending *habit* is highly developed in most Americans, but we know little of the more important *habit* of saving.... The habit of spending money is a mania with most people, and this habit keeps their noses to the grindstone al the days of their lives.

Saving or Spending. Which habit will be yours?

As you make this choice, keep in mind that Napoleon Hill's ideas about the importance of mastering money–instead of letting it master you–are echoed in the words of contemporary writers as well. In *The Courage to be Rich,* bestselling author Suze Orman notes:

> I have come to believe that the way each of us thinks and feels about our money is the key factor in determining how much money we ultimately have. The main underlying reason that some of us don't have money is that, with our thoughts and feelings about money have become internal obstacles that prevent us from having or keeping what we want. In the same vein, the reason that others do have money is that, with their thoughts and feelings, they have created the means to achieve and hold on to what they desire. In other words, out

thoughts and feelings about money are, to me, fundamental factors in determining how much money each of us will, in this lifetime, be able to create and keep.

And elsewhere in the same book, Orman says:
Over the years, I've heard from many people who think they don't have enough, that they will never have–or be–enough, that they can't get out of debt, can't provide for their children, can't face the future. I have heard tales of sadness, hopelessness, and despair from people facing the facts of the financial lives they have created. There is a vast difference between facing reality, bad as your particular financial reality might be at this moment, and thinking that you can't do anything about that reality. Whether you're wealthy, whether you're poor, the constricting thoughts that tell you that *you can't* are immensely powerful and terribly destructive. I have come to refer to them as thoughts of poverty, and thoughts of poverty can dwell in all of us, no matter how much or how little money we have. These thoughts of poverty are insidious; they lead to words of poverty or defeat, and ultimately to actions of poverty and a legacy of poverty that can be passed down for generations. We must learn to still those thoughts.

Orman goes on to relate the story of her father, a hardworking man who faced defeat over and over again in business:
It was not that my father was without

courage, for at least in my eyes, he had more than most; he had amazing courage. Despite this, my brothers and I heard him say, more than once, 'This is just the way it was meant to be, and there's nothing I can do about it.'

Finally, as an adult thinking back on what I knew of my father's life, I got it. No matter how hard he tried, his schemes never worked out for him because he never thought, deep down inside, that they could, never thought that they would. He thought he was never going to make it, thought it and thought it until he believed it, said it, and made it happen.

When you start a Habit of Saving, when you think and act as if you have control over your money, you are preventing this kind of powerful self-limitation. That ten dollars or fifty dollars or five hundred dollars that you set aside each month is a promise to yourself that money can work for you. It's a promise–and proof–that you can work for yourself. Starting small is no shame, but never starting...well, you know by now what you're saying to yourself.

Lesson Five
INITIATIVE AND LEADERSHIP

SUMMARY

The ability to recognize a problem or opportunity and take clear, effective steps to correct it has been a hallmark of the successful person since tribesmen first began telling stories of their ancestors around camp fires. The world has not changed all that much in the intervening millennia: proactive people inspire others to act accomplish things of lasting importance.

THE TEXT

Direct as ever, Napoleon Hill plunges right into the meat of his discussion:

All people may be placed in one or the other of two general classes. One is known as leaders and the other as followers. Rarely do the "followers" achieve noteworthy success, and they never succeed until they break away from the ranks of "followers" and become "leaders."

There is a mistaken notion being broadcast in the world among a certain class of people that a man is paid for that which he knows. This is only partly true, and, like other half truths, it does more damage than an out-and-out falsehood.

The truth is that a man is paid not only

for that which he *knows*, but more particularly for that which *he does* with what he knows, or, that which he *gets others to do.*

Without *initiative* no man will achieve success, no matter what he may consider success, because he will do nothing out of the ordinary run of mediocre work such as nearly all men are forced to do in order to have a place to sleep, something to eat, and clothes to wear. These three necessities may be had, of a certain kind, without the aid of *initiative* and *leadership*, but the moment a man makes up his mind to acquire more than the bare necessities of life, he must either cultivate the habits of *initiative* and *leadership* or else find himself hedged in behind a stone wall.

In short, to do more than get by, you have to put yourself forward and accomplish goals. To achieve what you want most out of life, you cannot simply fulfill expectations; you must exceed them. *Leadership and initiative are linked, but they are not the same thing.*

The Lack of Leadership

There are several types of people who struggle with this idea. Strangely, there are those who have certain leadership qualities, such as an ability to think independently and to chart their own paths through life. The trouble is, these folks are always butting heads with the people who set standards and make rules. They run the risk of spending more time arguing than they do accomplishing anything significant. They have initiative, but lack leadership.

Despite the idea of a leader as someone who makes his or her own rules, most leaders do not turn the whole world upside down in order to achieve their goals. Instead, they examine their circumstances, identify the major obstacle to their ambitions, and then they use as many of the other circumstances as possible to overcome the obstacle they face. People whose first instinct is to resist any standard or requirement have a hard time selecting their battles.

Knowing your purpose in life helps you set your priorities. Aware of your Definite Chief Aim, you can identify the next step to take, fight that battle, and win it, rather than taking on every challenge at once. Your energy is spent more effectively, and you gain the satisfaction that comes from every incremental success instead of feeling that the entire world is opposing you every moment of the day.

The comparison between all leaders and generals is obvious because there are few examples that show more directly how a leader selects a goal and uses other people to achieve it. A general who says "fire" and hopes for the best will lose to a general who defends his important positions, tries to advance where it is most useful, and uses his forces where they have an advantage. This is exactly how the French lost to the English at Potiers.

Leadership also implies the ability to convince and inspire people of the importance of your purpose. Working from initiative alone, you're liable to act as if the importance of your goal is obvious to everyone else, and to grow frustrated and angry with those who don't agree. Your goal is not equally important to others–that's why it is *your* goal. To lead, you have to devote time and effort to motivating and persuading others to take risks and make sacrifices.

Self-Confidence is essential to this facet of Leadership. You cannot hesitate or be half-hearted as you attempt to convince people to join you. You cannot let self-doubt hold you back from a course of action when you are asking others to depend on you to make decisions. In order to ask something extraordinary of others, you must be convinced of its value yourself and you must also know that the course you are setting is the right one.

Adding leadership to initiative is much simpler when you begin applying the Principles of Success. In addition to the lessons you've already studied, those on Enthusiasm, Cooperation and Tolerance will be especially helpful. But always keep in mind that a vision of what you want is not enough. You must have a plan and the ability to enlist others to work alongside you.

The Lack of Initiative

Another group who struggle to combine Initiative with Leadership are those who love rules and standards. These people like the notion of having a prescribed idea of excellence and quality, and they throw themselves into meeting every last requirement. But that's where they stop. The do exactly what is expected of them, and wonder why the world doesn't take more notice of them. Their trouble is that they do exactly what is expected of them, and *no more*.

These folks have the capacity to accomplish much, but they are never able to transform that capacity into something exceptional because they don't have the initiative to go beyond common expectations.

The lack of initiative doesn't mean that you turn in poor quality work, or that you fail at what you set out to do.

It's just that you don't ask yourself what would happen if you did more. You're paying more attention to the short-term than to the long-term, and you settle for the satisfactions of predictability.

Fears of various sorts are often behind this kind of dogged self-limitation. You know what you are good at. Why take a risk of failing at something? Why indeed? Are you perfectly happy now? Why are you reading this book?

If fears are stifling your initiative, keep in mind that you know that you are always capable of going back to what you know you do well. There is no true risk in reaching beyond and daring something new and bold. But there is the potential for enormous satisfaction, advancement and change is you try to apply your strengths to something fresh and exciting.

There is always a place in this world for people who do exactly what is expected of them. They are known quantities, and people who possess both initiative and leadership will know how to put them to work. But someone else will always be making the important decisions for those predictable types, and they will always be wondering if there's a way to get more out of life.

Once again, Self-Confidence is an important attribute to develop if you want to move on to cultivating initiative. You need to be able to act with a belief in yourself or you will always keep your talents in check. Later lessons on Enthusiasm, Imagination and even Profiting by Failure will serve you well.

Lesson Six
IMAGINATION

SUMMARY

Napoleon Hill's belief in the importance of imagination was unshakable. Most of the examples in this chapter are still with us in everyday life. The enduring quality of what people can achieve through imagination is a testament to the importance of this singular human ability. But just as significant is the way in which the use of imagination marks your achievements as something personal. That is to say, the use of imagination shows that you do not simply follow a formula for success: you create a success that is uniquely yours, sprung from your dreams and your heart and made real by your efforts.

THE TEXT

No man ever accomplished anything, ever created anything, ever built any plan or developed a definite chief aim without the use of his *imagination!*

Everything that any man ever created or built was first visioned, in his own mind, through *imagination!*

Years before it became a reality, the late John Wannamaker saw, in his own *imagination,* in practically all its details, the gigantic business which now bears his name and despite the fact that he was then without the capital to create such a business, he managed

77

to get it and to see the business he had
dreamed of in his mind become a splendid
reality.

Here, in his first example, Dr. Hill is drawing a direct
connection between imagination and the idea of a definite
chief aim. He makes clear to his readers that they already
possess this important skill because they have used it in
imagining their own success. Let there be no doubt in your
mind that you have imagination, as well.

There are popular stereotypes that say people such as
artists, actors and writers have more imagination than, say,
accountants, janitors and shopkeepers. This is wholly, utter-
ly false. Just because you have not yet begun to employ
your imagination to its fullest does not mean that you don't
have one. The key, as Dr. Hill will emphasize, is to use it
constructively. To sound a note you have heard before, you
will need to act to make the products of your imagination
become real.

In the workshop of the *imagination*, one
may take old, well-known ideas or concepts, or
parts of ideas, and combine them with still
other old ideas or parts of ideas, and out of
this combination create that which seems to be
new. This process is the major principle of all
invention.

One may have a *definite chief aim* and
a plan for achieving it; may possess *self-confidence* in abundance; may have a highly developed *habit of saving*, and both *initiative and
leadership* in abundance, but if the element of
imagination is missing, the other qualities will

be held useless, because there will be no driving force to shape the use of these qualities.
In the workshop of the imagination, all plans
are created, and without plans, no achievement is possible except by mere accident.

Dr. Hill underscores the significance of action in
pursuit of imagination's prompting. He quickly provides
two additional examples of men who built great
empires–not by letting their imaginations run away with
them, but by building upon a plan that imagination allowed
them to conceive. In both cases, there is more than a flash
of inspiration involved. A moment of insight is followed by
hard thinking and hard work.

Everyday Inspiration

Witness the manner in which *imagination* can be used as both the beginning and
the end of successful plans: Clarence
Saunders, who created the well-known chain
of Piggly-Wiggly grocery stores, conceived the
idea on which the stores were based, or rather
borrowed it, from the cafeteria restaurant system. While working as a grocer's helper, Mr.
Saunders went into a cafeteria for lunch.
Standing in line, waiting for his turn at the food
counters, the wheels of his imagination began
to turn, and he reasoned, to himself, something like this:

'People seem to like to stand in line and
help themselves. Moreover, I see that more

people can be served this way, with fewer salespeople. Why would it not be a good idea to introduce this plan in the grocery business, so people could come in, wander around with a basket, pick up what they wanted, and pay on the way out?'

Then and there, with that bit of elementary *"imagining,"* Mr. Saunders sowed the seed of an idea which later became the Piggly-Wiggly stores system and made him a multi-millionaire in the bargain.

Nearly a century after Clarence Saunders revolutionized the grocery store, we may laugh a little at the idea of waiting on a clerk to bring us a can of coffee or a dozen eggs. Retailing itself was fundamentally transformed by Saunders' ideas, to the point that it's hard for a modern shopper to imagine a time when all the merchandise was behind a counter. Where would Wal-mart or Victoria's Secret be in such a world?

Transformations such as this are not things of the past. Ask Michael Dell, founder of Dell Computers. As a high school student, Dell kept imagining better computers than companies like IBM were putting on the market. He'd already dismayed his parents by taking apart the first computer they bought him, but by putting it back together, and then adding components like additional memory, he'd improved it. His imagination was showing him something the big guys were missing

Soon Dell was customizing computers for his friends. His reputation for being able to build something better spread and he developed a circle of clients. During his freshman year of college, he spent so much time rebuilding computers that he knew where his future lay. He dropped out of school, opened his business, and Dell Computers was born.

In his memoir, *Direct from Dell,* Michael Dell provides an amazing account of how often imagination allowed his small company to grow. They had to find ways to sell their products, to build them less expensively, to provide powerfully effective customer service, and to keep giving themselves the technical edge that allowed them to grow. Dell Computers is no longer a small start-up where the boss brings breakfast donuts for the whole staff. Its position as a leading computer manufacturer depended on hard work, the willingness to take risks, and a commitment to high quality. But any reader of *Direct from Dell* will see just how important imagination has been in its phenomenal growth.

People like Clarence Saunders and Michael Dell force the rest of the world to change along with the ideas they introduce. No matter what the world looks like the day you first write down your definite chief aim and your plan for making it real, circumstances will change over time and some of those changes will affect the way in which you pursue your goals. Napoleon Hill's next example of powerful imagination illustrates this in a way he never envisioned when he wrote his words, but it's a significant reminder of how essential imagination is.

"Ideas" are the most profitable products of the human mind, and they are all created in the *imagination.* The five and ten cent store is the result of *imagination.* The system was created by F.W. Woolworth, and it "happened" in this way: Woolworth was working as a salesman in a retail store. The owner of the store complained that he had a considerable amount of old, unsaleable merchandise on hand that was in the way, and was about to throw some of it into the trash box to be consigned to the furnace, when Woolworth's *imagination* began to function.

'I have an idea,' said he, 'how to make this merchandise sell. Let's put it all on a table and place a big sign on the table saying that all articles will be sold at ten cents each.'

The idea seemed feasible; it was tried, worked satisfactorily, and then began further development which resulted, finally, in the big chain of Woolworth stores which belted the entire country and made the man who used his imagination a multimillionaire.

To a modern reader, the irony here is obvious. The great Woolworth chain is gone. Every store has been closed and only the ornate Woolworth Building in New York City remains to preserve the name of a man with a great imagination. What happened? A failure of imagination.

The market power that the Woolworth stores once had was usurped by a new generation of retail stores with names like Wal-mart and Kohls'. With F.W. Woolworth entombed in his Egyptian crypt, the company eventually lost touch with the creativity that had built it. In another seventy years, the names of current leaders may also be dim memories to our great-grandchildren, for imagination will always give upstarts–people like you, perhaps–a way to challenge the preeminence of those who have decided that the time has passed for a fresh look at the way things have always been done.

Imagination is an astoundingly powerful force, and it is available to anyone who seeks to use it. Dr. Hill realized that for anyone struggling to get by, imagination might seem more a means of escape than a tool to be taken up and used. And as long as you feed your imagination nothing more than fantasies, it can do no more than distract you with them.

Wielding imagination effectively requires two things from you. You need to become familiar enough with how it operates to recognize when it is providing you something useful, and you need to focus it on the task of achieving your definite chief aim. Dr. Hill, as usual, has some cogent suggestions:

> What is known as a "basic" patent is rarely offered for record at the Patent Office, meaning a patent that embraces really new and heretofore undiscovered principles. Most of the hundreds of thousands of patents applied for and granted every year, many of which are of a most useful nature, involve nothing more than a new arrangement or combination of old and well-known principles which have been used many times before in other ways and for other purposes.
>
> When Mr. Saunders created his famous Piggly-Wiggly stores system, he did not even combine two new ideas; he merely took an old idea that he saw in use *and gave it a new setting,* or in other words put it to a new use, but this required *imagination.*

To cultivate imagination so it will eventually suggest ideas of its own initiative, you should make it your business to keep a record of all the useful, ingenious and practical ideas you see in use in other lines of work outside your own occupation, as well as in connection with your own work. Start with an ordinary, pocket-size notebook, and catalogue every idea, or concept, or thought that occurs to you which is capable of practical use, and then take these ideas and work them into new plans. By and by the time will come when the powers of your own imagination will go into the storehouse of your subconscious mind, where all the knowledge you have ever gathered is stored, assemble this knowledge into new combinations, and hand over to you the results in the shape of *brand new ideas*, or what appear to be new ideas....

A single combination of ideas, which may be parts of old and well-known ideas, may be worth anywhere from a few cents to a few millions of dollars. Imagination is the one faculty on which there is no set price or value. It is the most important of the faculties of the mind, for it is here that all of a man's motives are given the impulse necessary to turn them into *action.*

The dreamer, who does nothing more than dream, uses imagination, but he falls short of utilizing this great faculty because he does not add to it the impulse to put his thoughts into *action.* Here is where *initiative* enters and goes to work for him, providing he is familiar with the Laws of Success and understands that ideas, of themselves, are worthless until put into action.

The dreamer who creates practical ideas must place back of these ideas three of the laws which have preceded this one, on *imagination*, namely:

1. The Law of A Definite Chief Aim
2. The Law of Self-Confidence
3. The Law of Initiative and Leadership

Without the influence of these three laws no man may put into action his thoughts and ideas, although the power to dream, imagine, and create may be highly developed.

Is it your business to succeed in life? How? That is something you must answer for yourself, but, in the main, you must proceed something after this order:

1. Adopt a definite purpose and create a definite plan for its attainment.
2. Take the initiative and begin putting your plan into action.
3. Back your initiative with belief in yourself and in your ability to successfully complete your plan.

No matter who you are, what you are doing, how much your income is, how little money you have, if you have a sound mind and if you are capable of using your imagination, you can gradually make a place for yourself that will command for you respect and give you all the worldly goods you need. There is no trick connected with this. The procedure is simple, as you may start with a very simple, elementary idea, plan, or purpose, and gradually develop it into something more pretentious.

Your *imagination* may not be sufficiently developed, at this time, to enable you to create some useful invention, but you can begin exercising this faculty by using it to create ways and means of improving the methods of performing your present work, whatever it may be. Your *imagination* will grow strong in proportion to the extent that you command it and direct it into use. Look about you and you will find plenty of opportunities to exercise your *imagination*. Do not wait for someone to show you what to do, but use vision and let your imagination suggest what to do. Do not wait for someone to pay you for using your imagination, because your real pay will come from the fact that every time you use it constructively in creating new combinations of ideas, it will grow stronger, and if you keep up this practice, the time will come, very soon, when your services will be sought eagerly, at any price within reason.

Imagine Your Own Promotion

If a man works in a gasoline filling station, for example, it may seem to him that he has but little range of opportunity to use his imagination. Nothing could be further from the real facts, for as a matter of fact, any man holding such a position may give his imagination the very finest sort of exercise by making it his business to cultivate every motorist whom he serves in such a manner that the motorist will come back for more service. Moreover, he may go a step further and work out ways and means of adding one new customer each day, or even one a week, or one a month, and in that manner very materially and quickly add to his income. Sooner or later, through this sort of exercise of his imagination, backed up by self-confidence and initiative, plus a definite chief aim, the man who follows this practice will be sure to create some new plan that will draw customers to his filling station from far and near, and he will then be on the great Highway to Success.

Dr. Hill's example of a gas station attendant is a model of how to use imagination that you have previously ignored. He suggests that the attendant focus on something concrete, a definable goal, and then spend time applying what his imagination suggests. Note that the concrete goal–a certain number of repeat customers in a fixed period–is not a world-changing ambition. It is, however, a goal that brings a benefit, and progress towards it is measurable, allowing the attendant to enjoy the satisfaction of seeing himself succeed at the use of the imagination. Larger, more ambitious visions become possible, and more likely, as the attendant becomes comfortable with the idea of using his imagination, and as his imagination is trained to seek out certain kinds of ideas.

As with so many other attributes of success, imagination amplifies itself. A little self-confidence allows you to attempt new things that build more self-confidence, and a little imagination creates situations which allow you to use even more imagination. Once you make the decision to give your imagination a focus, it will repay your determination very handsomely. "Imagination," said Albert Einstein, "is more important than knowledge."

No matter how unhappy you are with where you stand today, imagination will show you the way to overcome your obstacles and achieve the success you want.

Lesson Seven
ENTHUSIASM

SUMMARY

Enthusiasm is an obvious asset in pursuing your definite chief aim, but strangely enough, it has not been a recent vogue in motivational literature. Writers praise qualities such as determination, planning and teamwork, but they overlook the power and necessity of using this infectious attribute in accomplishing what you want most in life.

Napoleon Hill had no doubts about the value of enthusiasm, though his discussion of it in *The Ladder to Success* is brief. To his examples of its utility and importance we'll add some modern examinations of how enthusiasm can be used effectively, and provide you with some pointers on developing and channeling enthusiasm so that it serves your purposes.

THE TEXT

Enthusiasm is a driving force which not only gives greater power to the man who has it, but it is contagious and affects all whom it reaches. Enthusiasm over the work in which one is engages takes the drudgery out of that work. It has been observed that laborers, engaged in the toilsome job of ditch digging, can take the drabness out of their work by singing as they work.

When the "Yanks" went into action during the World War[3], they went in singing and full of enthusiasm. This was too much for the war-worn soldiers who had been in the field long enough to wear off their enthusiasm, and they made poor match indeed for the "Yanks."

The Filene Department Store, in Boston, is opened with music furnished by the store band every morning during the summer months. The sales people dance to the music, catch the rhythm of the tunes, and when the doors are finally opened for business the patrons of the store meet a jolly crowd of enthusiastic, cheerful, smiling sales people, many of whom are still softly humming the tune to which they had been dancing but a few minutes before. The spirit of enthusiasm remains with the salespeople throughout the day. It lightens their work and creates an "atmosphere" in the store which is pleasing to their customers.

This is a lesson which businesses seem to have learned in a strange fashion. Who can shop these days without the intrusion of canned music which has been chosen to heighten the mood of shoppers? Though it may seem quaint to imagine a "store band," the old Filene's had hit on something. They sought to influence their customers by influencing their salespeople. What would it be like to enter a store nowadays where the clerks were all upbeat, interested in

---

[3] When Napoleon Hill was writing, the phrase "World War" could mean only one conflict. Sadly, that is no longer the case, but it should be obvious from the date of the original book that he could only mean World War I.

their work, and happy to see you? Canned music is a hammer, as likely to backfire when shoppers hear songs they don't like, that are played too loudly for everyone's pleasure. An enthusiastic sales force is a precision tool, one which can interact with shoppers according to their needs and the moods they bring in off the street.

And here is a key element in the proper use of enthusiasm. Full-blown excitement is sometimes appropriate, and sometimes disastrous. The expression of enthusiasm is what truly counts. Burning inside you, it provides fuel for exertion, gives you the courage to try new things, and stiffens your resolve to face situations your fears tell you to avoid. You can reveal enthusiasm in a variety of ways. You can be grinning and energetic every moment of the day; sometimes that will be a boon, and sometimes it will be a disaster.

The Importance of Controlled Enthusiasm

Dr. Hill notes clearly:

Enthusiasm, to be of value, must be controlled and directed to definite ends. Uncontrolled enthusiasm may be, and generally is, destructive.

Imagine if, in a time of war, the President of the United States stood up before the nation and said, "We're gonna blow 'em to smithereens," and then laughed happily. The urge to conquer one's enemies is powerful at such time. An unenthusiastic pursuit of war would only prolong a terrible event and cost more lives than a swift and clean end. In the face of this knowledge, some citizens might applaud such a sentiment. But a greater number would be dismayed to hear a Commander-in-Chief speak so recklessly, with apparent joy in destruction. They would wonder if the war was being pursued for the sake of blowing things up, rather than for a just cause.

Recent events have shown us that a wise leader, while possessed of all the necessary enthusiasm for conducting a war, must always temper that enthusiasm with the gravity of the situation and an awareness of the risks and costs. Instead of displaying wild jubilation, the leader must convey a sense of determination and steadfastness.

The odds that you will be leading a nation into war are blessedly small. But in any situation, you must judge your goal and your audience, and attune your actions accordingly. Doing so aligns your enthusiasm with your purpose. It tells you whether you need spontaneity or determined adherence to a long-range plan. If you need to alter the mood of the people you are dealing with, it allows you to start from a common point, even if what you aim to achieve is a complete reversal of the current feeling.

A certain amount of practice is always necessary in order to become a good judge of other people's moods. Beginning cautiously is good, at least until you reach the point where your initial reading of a situation seems to be reliable. Keep in mind, though, that controlled enthusiasm is in no way diminished enthusiasm. As you give your enthusiasm a consistent focus, you will find that it grows stronger from its successes.

If you find it difficult to summon enthusiasm at will for the tasks you face, take the time to examine things that you do approach with enthusiasm. Perhaps it is a hobby, or simply another aspect of your job that you pursue without prompting. Is there something you lose yourself in, and do with assurance? Is there something you tackle despite the fear of failure or unpleasant reactions? You've found something you do with enthusiasm.

Dr. Hill had a notion of one common, human activity that most people pursue with great enthusiasm:

> The acts of so-called "bad boys" are nothing more nor less than uncontrolled enthusiasm. The wasted energy of uncontrolled enthusiasm expressed though promiscuous sexual contact, and sex desire not expressed through contact, by the majority of young men, is sufficient to lift them to high achievement if this urge were harnessed and transformed to some other form of physical action.

Think about the way in which people pursue sex. We focus all our energy into it, we consider the way we present ourselves, and we adjust our approach to the situation. When we aren't in a position to achieve our goals quickly, we're still considering how we might better our chances, thinking about a trip to the gym, some new clothes, or anything else we might try to improve the odds. We might even devote a great deal of mental power to picturing ourselves enjoying what we wanted–and find that our enthusiasm for it only grows more intense.

Imagine, then, if your enthusiasm for sex was matched by an enthusiasm for your definite chief aim. Or if not sex, whatever it is that is always bubbling away on the back burner of your mind. Wouldn't you like to have that kind of focused pursuit of your other goal in life?

You can achieve this kind of controlled enthusiasm.

Without eliminating your desire for whatever it is that brings you joy, you can make it a point, as soon as you become conscious that your secondary priority is occupying your mind, to shift your thinking to your definite chief aim. At first, this will seem a labor and you may feel like a killjoy. But you are not in danger of this.

As you begin to focus your enthusiasm on your definite chief aim, you will gain many benefits. Self-confidence and initiative will come more easily. Your imagination will be more fertile. You will increase your ability to tap into the powers of your Master Mind alliance. Even your determination to save money will be stronger. Progress toward your definite chief aim will begin to animate you in a way you never felt before. And whatever it is you seek for more immediate satisfaction will come more readily to someone with all these assets.

With controlled enthusiasm working for you, you will always find a way to make yourself equal to the task at hand. That ability will not come overnight, but you will know with certainty that you can create it. That knowledge is priceless.

Lesson Eight
SELF-CONTROL

SUMMARY

As the lesson on Enthusiasm has just made clear, the ability to consciously channel your energy and effort toward your definite chief aim is essential. Though Self-Control has been a part of earlier lessons (Habit of Saving, Enthusiasm), it is important enough that Napoleon Hill treats it separately.

The greatest threat to Self-Control is unbridled emotion. Taking command of your emotions is not the same thing as eliminating them, though you can, through careful choices, so weaken certain unwanted emotional responses that they will cease to have any real impact. Conversely, you can encourage healthy emotional responses, and by doing so, gain an enormous advantage in your pursuit of success.

THE TEXT

(The opening paragraphs of this lesson are more easily understood when you know that when Dr. Hill refers to the "suprarenal" glands, or simply to "suprarenal," he means adrenaline. The word "suprarenal" is derived from the position of these glands just above the kidneys.)

Lack of Self-Control has brought grief to more people than any other shortcoming known to the human race. This evil shows itself, at one time or another, in every person's life.

Every successful person must have some sort of balance wheel for his or her emotions. When a person "loses his temper," something takes place in his brain which should be better understood. When a person becomes extremely angry, the suprarenal glands begin to empty their contents into the blood, and if this is kept up for any great length of time, the amount will be sufficient to do serious damage to the entire system, sometimes resulting in death.

Suprarenal is Nature's "repair kit" with which she causes the blood to coagulate and stop the flow in the event of injury. Anger immediately excites the suprarenal glands, and their contents begin to pour into the blood. This accounts for one turning white and red in the face, alternately, as the flow of blood throughout the body is temporarily checked. No doubt Nature created this system for man's protection during the savage state of his development, when anger usually preceded a terrific fight with some other savage, which might mean opening of the veins and loss of blood.

The release of adrenaline is part of the fight-or-flight response to stress. The human body prepares for quick action, including possible injury, by a release of energy and the restriction of blood flow to the skin's surface. Breathing becomes more rapid to provide more oxygen to muscles, either for running or some other action. While useful in "savage" times, the adrenaline response is still important whenever you need to respond quickly to a physical threat, such as a slip on the ice.

An indirect threat can also trigger an adrenaline reaction. The famous example out of urban folklore is the mother who lifts something very heavy (even a car) off a child. In both kinds of situations, the adrenaline rush is triggered by a signal from the brain, and it is, very basically, an emotional response.

Hardwired for Failure?

Unfortunately, the adrenaline response can assume a life of its own. A peaceful person who is suddenly injured may lash out as inhibitions are lowered for the sake of acting quickly. Hit your finger with a hammer while driving a nail and you may use language you don't usually resort to, or you may fling the hammer away (and cause more damage).

In the August, 1920 issue of *Hill's Golden Rule*, a magazine Dr. Hill edited in Chicago, he provided an even more dramatic example:

On our way to the office this morning we saw an accident which reminded us how well it pays to develop the wonderful ability of self-control.

A man stepped off the sidewalk without looking to right or left, and a passing automobile nearly clipped his coat-tail.

He trotted along after the machine, shaking his fist at the driver and swearing to avenge himself if he caught up with the automobile.

While chasing away one hazard another one came up

on his off side in the shape of a street car, and struck him a blow which rendered him unconscious.

This is a very simple example of the way in which an emotional response–which comes very quickly–can have unwanted, potentially harmful effects. We've all had experiences where, in the heat of the moment, we did or said something uncharacteristic and greatly regretted it.

The answer is not the elimination of emotion. We need the adrenaline response just as much as we need joy and sadness and even appropriate anger. Complete stifling of emotion would render you inert–why bother to eat, or work if nothing had any significance for you?

It's rare that an emotional reaction triggers a response as immediate as cursing when you hit yourself with a hammer. Most of the time, we have a lag of seconds or minutes or hours, in which we evaluate our situation and then choose to act. And the question is then whether we act in the grip of emotion, or in a reasoned way that works to our benefit.

There is an exhilaration that comes with adrenaline, a feeling of energy and an urge to act that is compelling. Most of the time, the urge is simply to eliminate the threat, and the temptation is to lash out, physically or verbally. Yet it's obvious that this response can easily lead to escalation and further danger.

It's in those first moments that we need to exercise Self-Control. Tame the response and the adrenaline rush recedes. It becomes easier to think and reason, to evaluate actual and potential harm, and to choose a course of action that repairs or prevents further harm. The struggle for Self-Control is not really a day-long battle over one's emotions so much as it is a matter of thinking before acting. That is,

Self-Control is a series of small, brief assertions of will-power that add up.

Rage is not the only emotion that one needs to rein in this way. We each have our weaknesses. When we turn to food for comfort, we lose that brief battle for Self-Control over despair or self-pity. When we procrastinate, we fail to assert ourselves over fear.

Any emotional response that you allow to get the better of you is delaying your progress toward your definite chief aim. The old approach of counting to ten before you act is often enough of a distraction to help you assert your will-power, but if you find that this fails you, then it might be appropriate to ask yourself some deeper questions about why your emotions rule you as they do. Seek help if you cannot master your emotional responses. Talk to friends or family, a member of the clergy or a professional counselor. Where is the shame in trying to improve yourself? Any embarrassment you feel cannot be worse than the frustration of constant self-sabotage.

Consider instead the satisfaction of coming to understand that your actions are moving you forward rather than holding you back. If you train yourself so that you stop and rationally analyze surprises rather than simply lashing out; if you master your urges to indulge in things that are frivolous or unhealthy; if you treat the pursuit of your definite chief aim as the most important and satisfying action in your life, then you have control not only over your thoughts and actions, but over your destiny itself.

Lesson Nine
THE HABIT OF DOING MORE
THAN YOU ARE PAID FOR

SUMMARY

Here is another one of Dr. Hill's distinctive ideas that has not been readily embraced by other well-known writers. But as he makes very clear, this special kind of effort brings two important rewards: improved skill and a better reputation. The lesson is short, but the opportunities for applying it would make up a long list, indeed.

THE TEXT

This law is a stumblingblock on which many a promising career has been shattered. There is a general attitude among people to perform just as little service as they can get by with, but if you will study these people carefully, you will observe that while they may be actually "getting by" temporarily, they are not, however, getting anything else.

There are two major reasons why all successful people must practice this Law, as follows:

1. Just as an arm or a limb of the body grows strong in exact proportion to its use, so does the mind grow strong through use. By

100

rendering the greatest possible amount of service, the faculties through which the service is rendered are put into use and, eventually, become strong and accurate.

2. By rendering more service than that for which you are paid, you are turning the spotlight of *favorable* attention upon yourself, and it will not be long before you will be sought with fancy offers for your services, and there will be a continuous market for those services.

'Do the thing and you shall have the power,' was the admonition of Emerson, the great modern philosopher.

That is literally true! Practice makes perfect. The better you do your work, the more adept you become at doing it, and this, in time, will lead to such perfection that you will have few, if any equals in your field of endeavor.

The idea of doing more than your job description entails was brought home to Dr. Hill very early in his professional life, at the first office job he held. As he wrote in *Hill's Golden Rule*:

...a few months later, I learned that it pays to be on the lookout constantly for the opportunity to perform work which one is not really paid to perform. The auditor's desk was next to mine. He thought it was a good joke on me because I would come back evenings and perform certain routine work for him, such as checking bills, posting ledgers and the like. This gave him more time to "do society."

One day he went away-or, one night, I believe it was and never showed up again. The payrolls had not been made up and it was almost payday. I knew how to complete his unfinished work on the payrolls because I had been doing this work for him during my spare time, and of evenings when he was out with his best girl, therefore I went ahead, without being invited to do so, and finished his uncompleted work.

Down at the bottom of the payroll sheet was a blank for the auditor to sign his name, certifying that he had checked the payroll extensions and that they were correct. When the payrolls went to the "big chief's" office my name was on that line, as Auditor, without anyone having given me that title or asked me to perform that work.

My name was on the same line every month thereafter until I was promoted into a better position. I got the auditor's job by learning how to do his work on my own time without being expected to do it or paid for it.

Although he is emphasizing the habit of doing more than you are paid for, Dr. Hill is also making a case here for the importance of initiative. These two qualities often operate together, for by seeking to deliver the best possible service, you are attempting to address issues and concerns that are not normally your responsibility. Applied with the habit that is the subject of this lesson, initiative brings you improved skills as well as reputation for being someone who gets things done. This kind of reputation means that you will be asked to get other things done, with all the opportunities for self-improvement and attention that come with new challenges.

There's no doubt that embracing this attitude will require hard work and imagination. And it would only be fair to point out that the rewards you receive from others for doing more than you are paid to do may not add up, in a strict sense, to the amount of effort you expend. But keep in mind that you are compensating yourself through increased skills. You should also keep in mind the Law of Increasing Returns. Dr. Hill taught that any effort, good or bad, sets in motion a chain of events which amplify its results over the long term. "As you sow," the Bible says, "so shall you also reap."

By rendering more service and better service than that for which you are paid, you thereby take advantage of the Law of Increasing Returns through the operation of which you will eventually be paid, in one way or another, for far more service than you actually perform.

This is no mere finely spun theory. It actually works out in the most practical tests. You must not imagine, however, that the Law always works instantaneously. You may render more service and better service than you are supposed to render for a few days, then discontinue the practice and go back to the old, ususal habit of doing as little as can be safely trusted to get you by, and the results will in no way benefit you. But adopt the habit as a part of your life's philosophy, and let it become well known by all who know you that you render such service out of choice, not as a matter of accident, but by *deliberate intent,* and soon you will see keen competition for your service.

You may not find very many people rendering such service, which is all the better for you, because you will stand out in bold contrast with practically all others who are engaged in work similar to yours. Contrast is a powerful law, and you may, in this manner, profit by contrast.

No Instant Payoff

If it hasn't been your habit to do more than you are paid to do and, in truth, you've made an art of doing as little as possible, you may find that the starkest contrast is between your old self and the new one. This is an advantageous change, but do not be discouraged if it seems to take some time before everyone trusts your new attitude. For some while, the Law of Increasing Returns will still be bringing home to you the results of all your efforts to just get by. It takes many good example to undo a history of slacking. Yet even during those days when it seems the spotlight of favorable attention doesn't even know you exist, you are still benefitting from your new habit by strengthening your skills and learning new things. And, of course, there is the straightforward benefit of building your devotion to one of the principles of Success.

Cynicism will suggest that the habit of doing more

than you are paid for is a fast way to exhaust yourself. Why shouldn't you be applying your time and energy to your own ends, instead of to the benefit of others? Isn't this a dog-eat-dog world, in which only the strongest and fittest survive?

No, actually. We live in a market society in which people trade goods and services they do have for things they do not have. Those who always insist on driving what appears to be the sharpest bargain may feel they are profiting the most, but they'll discover that few people look forward to doing business with them. Traders eager for business make it a point to let their customers know they are getting something extraordinary. Those customers come back.

No matter what your goal in life may be, the rest of the world is your market. Even if you are not actually selling something, you will need cooperation, attention, and help from other people. The surest way to get this is to embrace the habit of doing more than you are paid for.

Careful study of the lives of successful men has shown that faithfully practicing this one Law alone has brought the usual emoluments in which success is measured in plentiful quantities. If this author of this philosophy has to choose one of the Seventeen Laws of Success as being the most important, he would, without a moment's hesitation, chose this law of *Rendering More Service and Better Service than You are Paid for.*

Lesson Ten
PLEASING PERSONALITY

SUMMARY

The ability to create and maintain a good impression of yourself in the minds of other people smooths over many of the bumps in the road to success. It can also mean the difference between inspiring antagonism or cooperation in people, whether you have just met them or have known them for years.

Entire books have been devoted to presenting a pleasing personality to the world. Dr. Hill was not the first to recognize the significance of this idea; as far back as the fourteenth century, writers were advising those who sought success on how to conduct themselves. But in *The Ladder to Success,* Dr. Hill offers a succinct course in behaving in a manner that is more than a facade. By following his advice, you transform yourself so that all your best characteristics are on display to the people you meet and hope to influence.

THE TEXT

By most accounts, Dr. Hill was a man whose own personality registered very well. He was already in retirement when he was persuaded to come to Chicago to offer a speech to a civic group. As soon as the speech was completed, one of Chicago's most successful business leaders strode up to Dr. Hill and laid out a plan–inspired by Dr. Hill's speech–for renewing the enterprise of spreading the philosophy laid out in this book.

This was a significant commitment for W. Clement Stone, founder and chairman of Combined Insurance. Mr. Stone was long familiar with Dr. Hill's ideas and had employed them in training his salespeople, but the impression that Dr. Hill made in a single appearance was so powerful that Mr. Stone knew that he had to persuade the author to work alongside him. It says something about Mr. Stone's personality that Dr. Hill, well into his sixties and contemplating enjoying the fruits of his labors, quickly agreed.

A Pleasing Personality does not work miracles. If Dr. Hill had not created a proven philosophy, and if Mr. Stone had not tested its ideas himself, the two men would have never embarked on their enthusiastic collaboration. But the commitment of resources on Mr. Stone's part, and time and energy on the part of Dr. Hill, would have been impossible if both men had not possessed the kind of personality that inspires trust and confidence.

Dr. Hill offers a host of details that go into creating a Pleasing Personality:

A Pleasing Personality, naturally, is a personality that does not antagonize.

Personality cannot be defined in one word, nor in half a dozen words, for it represents the sum total of all of one's characteristics, good and bad.

Your Personality is totally unlike any other personality. It is the sum total of the qualities, emotions, characteristics, appearances, etc., which distinguish you from all other people on earth.

Your clothes form an important part of your personality; the way you wear them, the harmony of the colors you select, the quality and many other details all go to indicate much that belongs distinctly as a part of your personality. The psychologists claim that they can accurately analyze any person, in many important respects, by turning that person loose in a clothing store where there is a great variety of clothing, with instructions to select whatever may be wanted and dress in the clothes selected.

Your facial expression, as shown by the lines of your face, or lack of lines, forms an important part of your personality. Your voice, its pitch, tone, volume, and the language you use form important parts of your personality, because they mark you instantly, as a person of refinement, or the opposite.

The manner in which you shake hands constitutes an important part of your Personality. If, when shaking hands, you merely hold out a cold "hunk" of flesh and bones that is limp and lifeless, you are displaying a sign of a personality that is not mixed with *enthusiasm* or *initiative*.

A Pleasing Personality usually may be found in a person who speaks gently and kindly, selecting refined words that do not offend, in a modest tone of voice; who selects clothing of appropriate style and colors which harmonize; who is unselfish and not only willing but desirous of serving others; who is a friend of all humanity, the rich and the poor alike, regardless of politics, religion, or occupation; who refrains from speaking unkindly of others, either with or without cause; who manages to converse without being drawn into vulgar conversations or useless arguments on such debatable subjects as politics and religion; who sees both the good and the bad in people, but makes due allowance for the latter; who seeks neither to reform nor to reprimand others; who smiles frequently and deeply; who loves music and little children; who sympathizes with all who are in trouble and forgives acts of unkindness; who willingly grants to others the right to so as they please so long as no one's rights are interfered with; who earnestly strives to be constructive in every thought and deed indulged in; who encourages others and spurs them on to greater and better achievement in their chosen line of work.

What an amazing list! You could probably add to it yourself if you considered all the qualities that you find admirable in others. You should display every element of this list yourself, though Dr. Hill is careful to point out that every personality is unique. Still, it may seem a little daunting to imagine incorporating all these characteristics into your behavior.

Growing Your Personality

Fortunately, many of these qualities will become evident in your actions as you learn and apply the lessons in

Dr. Hill's writing. Enthusiasm brings a smile to your face often; initiative firms up your handshake, and the habit of doing more than you are paid to do gives you a service-oriented outlook. In lessons to come, you'll find that living by the Golden Rule inspires tolerance, profiting from failure (and experiencing a few) inspires compassion, and accurate thinking sharpens your vocabulary and makes you speech effective.

And this is all to the good. A Pleasing Personality must be based on actual attitudes. You would go mad trying to adjust your personality all the time if its most significant aspects were not part of your nature. How, then, do you correct a flaw which is evident in your personality?

The key is to begin acting as if you already possess the trait you desire. While this may seem like a charade, it is not–if your primary purpose is to inspire the creation of the attitude in yourself. Some people might regard this as sophistry, but consider someone whose vocabulary is weak. If that person makes an effort to learn new words and apply them correctly, who can find a fault there? Similarly, if you're at first brusque in dealing with others, and then you make a concerted effort to treat them with respect, who can complain of the improvement? A nit-picker might say your attitude is a sham, but if you act on it repeatedly, it will become a habit and as much a part of you as your old habit of being rude.

Nearly every aspect of a Pleasing Personality is simply a habit, and like all habits, these aspects are self-reinforcing. Curse frequently and you will curse more. Smile often and you will smile more. It takes discipline, as you know, to create new habits, but this is something you are already acquiring as you embrace the principles of success:

The development of a Pleasing Personality calls for the exercise of Self-Control, because there will be many incidents and many people to try your patience and destroy your good resolutions to become pleasing. The reward is worthy of the effort, however, because one who possesses a Pleasing Personality stands out so boldly in contrast with the majority of people around him, that his pleasing qualities become all the more pronounced.

Your dream of success may hinge on ideas of independence and freedom of expression. Cultivating a Pleasing Personality may seem a distraction for you, almost a step backwards if you are of a particularly independent bent. It is not. No matter what you hope to accomplish, you will need the goodwill and aid of other people. Learning habits that will inspire that good feeling can never hold you back, for by instilling the characteristics of a Pleasing Personality in yourself, you are equipping yourself with skills–enthusiasm, initiative, accurate thinking, inspiring cooperation, and tolerance among others–that are essential to anyone's chances of success.

A Pleasing Personality is not window dressing. It can only be created through embracing attitudes and habits everyone needs. You will not lose yourself in the new personality you forge; rather, you will define yourself–your successful self–in terms of exactly what and who you wish to be.

Lesson Eleven
ACCURATE THINKING

SUMMARY

Every plan for success is fluid; it must constantly take into account the progress you are making, the defeats you suffer, and new information which pours in from the world at large. To calculate your progress, discover the reasons for your setbacks, and overcome obstacles which arise unforeseen, you need Accurate Thinking.

An incorrect assessment can cost you time, money, happiness and opportunity. Learning to evaluate the flood of stimuli which you experience in daily life is a skill that grows through constant employment. There is mental-and sometimes physical- labor involved–in reaching an accurate conclusion, but the effort always pays off.

THE TEXT

Dr. Hill proceeds as directly as ever toward laying out his ideas:

The art of Accurate Thinking is not difficult to acquire, although certain definite rules must be followed. To think accurately, one must follow at least two basic principles:

1. Accurate Thinking calls for the separation of facts from mere information.

2. *Facts*, when ascertained, must be separated into two classes; one is known as *important* and the other as *unimportant* or irrelevant.

The question naturally arises, "What is an *important fact?*" and the answer is, "An *important fact* is any fact essential for the attainment of one's definite major purpose, or which may be useful or necessary in connection with one's daily occupation. All other facts, while they may be useful and interesting, are comparatively unimportant as far as the individual is concerned."

No man has the right to have an opinion on any subject, unless he has arrived at that opinion by a process of reasoning that is based on all the available *facts* connected with the subject of the opinion. Despite this fact, however, nearly everyone has opinions on nearly every subject, whether or not they are familiar with those subjects or have and *facts* connected with them.

This last paragraph is a very broad and seemingly intemperate idea that may strike you as overly strong. "This is a free country!" some may cry. "We have a right to opinions! All the opinions we want! Even several on the same subject!"

Dr. Hill, however, is writing forcefully in order to caution, not condemn. There is danger in unsupported opinion, which comes from both those opinions you have on your own and from those which are offered so freely by those around you.

Snap judgments and opinions that are not opinions at all, but mere wild conjectures or guesses, are valueless; "there's not an *idea* in a carload" of them. Any man may become an Accurate Thinker by making it his business to insist on getting the Facts, all that are available with reasonable effort, before reaching decisions or creating opinions on any subject.

When you hear a man begin a discourse with such generalities as "I hear that so and so is the case," or "I see by the papers that so and so did so and so," you may put that man down as one who *is not* an Accurate Thinker, and his opinions, guesses, statements, and conjectures, should be accepted, if at all, with a good big handful of the proverbial salt of caution.

The danger in heeding unsupported opinions is, quite obviously, that they may well not be true. They do not represent anything useful to you. Yet they are perniciously prevalent, and it is impossible to go through the day without being assailed with them. Cab drivers, office mates, sales clerks, and the guy in front of you at the grocery store may all have something to tell you, but you simply cannot make decisions on the basis of what you hear.

Does this seem obvious? Perhaps, but all the freefloating opinions in the world create a kind of community mindset that is reflected back on you in the course of the day. Without challenging yourself to examine all that you hear and read, you run the serious risk of becoming a mirror of received wisdom. You cannot make your plan for success come true on the basis of the status quo. You are out to change that status quo, and to do it, you must be able to identify the errors in the group thinking.

Where would Michael Dell be if he had accepted the idea that established computer companies knew how to provide what their customers wanted? What would Dr. Martin Luther King have accomplished if he had not been willing to dream of a different America? Where would medicine be without the likes of Pasteur and Jenner and their willingness to examine common assumptions. Einstein, Picasso, and Frank Lloyd Wright all achieved their greatness by Accurate Thinking in the face of erroneous ideas. So will you.

There is, however, a price.

Accuracy is Never Free

It often requires considerable effort to *know facts* on any subject, which is perhaps the main reason why so few people take the time or go to the trouble to gather *facts* as the basis for their opinions.

You are presumably following this philosophy for the purpose of learning how you may become more successful, and if that is true then *you* must break away from the common practices of the masses who do not think and take the time to gather *facts* as the basis of your thoughts. That this requires effort is freely admitted, but it must be kept in mind that *success* is not something that one may come along and pluck from a tree, where it has grown of its own accord. Success is something that represents perseverance, self-sacrifice, determination, and strong character.

Everything has its price, and nothing

may be obtained without paying this price; or, if something of value is obtained, it cannot be retained for long. The price of Accurate Thinking is the effort required to gather and organize the *facts* on which to base the *thought.*

If these words seem intimidating, keep in mind that they apply only to what is important to you. You do not need to approach every topic with the rigor that you devote to your definite chief aim. Unless your goal requires it, you do not need an opinion on the great questions of history or the issues which face the nation. A person could spend eternity trying to get all the facts on every question. Concentrate on matters pertaining to your definite chief aim.

This may, suggest, however, that the next time your neighbor starts a discussion of a local political race, you think hard before you offer an "opinion" of your own. Once aquired, Accurate Thinking is a hard habit to break, and examining assumptions you have already made can be an education in itself. An Accurate Thinker looks past old ideas to find new ones to his or her profit.

Dr. Hill closes his discussion of Accurate Thinking with just such an example. He returns, once again, to the scene of a humble gas station:

'How many automobiles pass this filling station each day,' the manager of a chain of filling stations asked a new service man. 'And on what days is traffic the heaviest?'

'I am of the opinion...' the young man began.

'Never mind your *opinion*,' the manager

interrupted. 'What I asked you for calls for an answer based upon *facts*. Opinions are worth nothing when actual *facts* are obtainable.'

With the aid of a pocket adder this young man began to count the automobiles that passed his station each day. He went a step further and recorded the number that actually stopped and purchased supplies, giving the figures day by day for two weeks, including Sundays.

Nor was this all! He estimated the number of automobiles that should have stopped at his station for supplies, day by day, for two weeks. Going still further, he created a plan that cost only a one cent postal card per motorist, that actually increased the number of automobiles that stopped at his station for service the following two weeks. This was not part of his required duties, but the question asked him by his manager had put him to *thinking,* and he made up his mind to profit by the incident.

The young man in question is now a half owner in a chain of filling stations of his own, and a moderately wealthy man, thanks to his ability to become an Accurate Thinker.

Opportunity is not seen by everyone, or everyone would be successful. Accurate Thinking is not simply insurance against mistakes, it's the key to knowing when and where to apply your efforts. The days of the one cent post card are long past, but Accurate Thinking remains as the tool of anyone who seeks something better out of life.

Lesson Twelve
CONCENTRATION

SUMMARY

Concentration is focusing your efforts on the pursuit of your definite chief aim. This may seem an obvious point, but it bears stressing for several reasons. First, you gain the ability to hone all your skills and knowledge so that they serve you in pursuit of your definite chief aim. Second, it reminds you of the importance of employing a Master Mind, for there are very few people who can be successful completely on their own. And third, a little success can sometimes be a dangerous thing.

THE TEXT

Dr. Hill steps up at the beginning of the chapter with more frank advice:

> The jack-of-all-trades seldom accomplished much at any trade. Life is so complex, and there are so many ways of dissipating energy unprofitably, that the habit of *concentrated effort* must be formed and adhered to by all who succeed.
>
> Power is based upon organized effort or energy. Energy cannot be organized without the habit of *concentration* of all the faculties on one thing at a time. An ordinary reading glass may be used to so focus the rays of the sun

that they will burn a hole in a board in a few minutes. Those same rays will not even heat the board until they are *concentrated* on one spot.

The human mind is something like a reading glass, because it is the medium through which all the faculties of the brain may be brought together and made to function, in co-ordinated formation, just as they rays of the sun may be focused on one spot with the aid of a reading glass.

It is worthy of serious consideration to remember that all the outstanding men of suc-cess, in all walks of life, concentrated the major portion of their thoughts and efforts upon one *definite purpose*, objective, or *chief aim*.

Dr. Hill then enters into a lengthy list of successful men of the day. Most of their names are still very well known to us: Henry Ford, Marshall Field, Wrigley, Edison, George Eastman of Eastman Kodak, Carnegie, Orville Wright, Marconi, Woodrow Wilson, John D. Rockefeller, Abraham Lincoln, and William Randolph Hearst.

Dr. Hill was making it crystal clear to his readers that whether they are in business, industry, science or politics, concentration is essential to accomplishing anything signif-icant. A modern day list might look like this:

- Oprah Winfrey, who concentrated on being the most successful talk show host;
- Bill Gates, who concentrated on making Windows the dominant computer operating system;
- Michael Eisner, who concentrated on remaking the

Disney corporation into a media empire;
- Ted Turner, who concentrated on turning one television station into a national network;
- Jeff Bezos, who concentrated on making Amazon the number one Internet retailer;
- Ralph Lauren, who concentrated on making himself a household name in fashion;
- James Cameron, who concentrated on making Titanic the most successful movie ever;
- Craig Venter, who concentrated on mapping the human genome;
- J.K. Rowling, who concentrated on writing the Harry Potter novels and made them a worldwide phenomenon;
- Thomas Keller, who concentrated on making his French Laundry restaurant the most respected in America;
- Orville Redenbacher, who concentrated on perfecting popcorn and made a fortune from a humble food.

You can probably add a dozen names to this list with a few moments of thought. Most well-known people are famous because they have concentrated their efforts in the pursuit of a single, clearly-defined goal, and stuck to that pursuit. There are, of course, famous people who have parlayed success in one arena into success in another. Ronald Reagan, a notable actor before he became president, is a good example. But remember that such people have learned to succeed once and begun again. When was the last time you heard of someone who was still struggling to achieve his or her original dream, but made it big doing something else?

Concentrate to Maximize

Concentrated effort does not mean literally doing one thing, and only one thing. Just as Oprah Winfrey does not simply talk on camera and enjoy the highest rated talk show in the country, you will have to be active on many fronts in order to achieve success. But Winfrey isn't running around her studio positioning the lights and cameras, or making travel arrangements for her guests, either. She concentrates her energies on aspects of her job like guest selection and interviewing skills, and chooses effective people to handle the other work.

You'll see here how the Master Mind principle is essential to concentration. Finding good people to work with allows you to engage in concentrated effort that maximizes your strengths–and the strengths of others–for highly effective results. Can you imagine if Oprah Winfrey tried to book a hotel room for a guest herself? She'd spend hours while the reservation agents gushed with the excitement of talking to her. It wouldn't be productive in the slightest.

A Master Mind also allows you to put people with specific talents to work on jobs for which you lack talent. James Cameron might, with years of training, be a fine actor, but he concentrates on producing and directing and leaves the acting to people who have made a career of it. Michael Eisner does not insist on drawing animations for Disney films. Ralph Lauren does not take the pictures for his advertising campaigns.

Yet all of these people, through concentration, shape the nature of the work that is done for them by others. Thomas Keller does not cook every dish that ends up on the tables at the French Laundry, but his dedication to his goals allows him to convey to his line cooks exactly what he expects of them. They don't have to ask themselves, "Would the chef think this looks good on the plate?" They know what Keller would think because of the example he sets by his own concentrated effort in the kitchen. Meanwhile, Keller is developing new dishes for his guests while others stock the wine cellar, take reservations, and train the wait staff–all to standards set by the chef's concentrated effort.

All of these successful people–like anyone who has risen to the top of his or her profession–have gone beyond just getting by. They have focused their energies on high goals, and attained them by keeping their focus there. While this may seem to be an obvious necessity, the ugly truth is that a smattering of success can be a terrible distraction. Many people discover that improved cash flow and increased respect from friends, family, and colleagues is quite nice. They then proceed to forget the larger goal that drove them to acquire all this.

People who find themselves stalled in what seemed to have been a promising journey toward success usually have this kind of thinking to blame. They feel good about what they have accomplished, at least for a while, and then dissatisfaction sets in. Sometimes the hunger for success reawakens in them and they begin to concentrate their efforts once more.

The worst result is that they begin to feel they simply do not have all the trappings of success that they should, and they spend themselves silly buying fancy new toys to distract themselves from feelings of failure. Or they may seek other diversions that compromise their health and self-respect, along with the modest paraphernalia that led them into mistaking progress toward a goal for its attainment.

This is not to say that you may not reevaluate your goals in life and choose new ones. There are plenty of worthy reasons for such reassessment. Yet if you do make such a choice, be sure that you are not simply rationalizing a desire to take it easy. Choose your new ambition with enthusiasm, and pursue it with the same concentrated effort you put into your former goal.

Of course there are also many people for whom success is still just an idea. There's always one more thing that needs to be taken care of before they really get down to tackling their definite chief aim. The kids need to start school or finish school before there's enough time. The car has to be replaced before saving can become a priority. A Pleasing Personality won't be necessary until they get that new job and can start afresh.

None of these people are concentrating, and none of them have what they really want. Neither will you, until you begin to concentrate.

Lesson Thirteen
COOPERATION

SUMMARY

Throughout *The Ladder to Success,* Dr. Hill has emphasized the need to work with other people. The lessons on the Master Mind, Enthusiasm, Initiative and Leadership, and Pleasing Personality all stress the importance of working relationships. So, it is no surprise that cooperation forms an essential step on *The Ladder to Success.*

Cooperation[4] has to be given to be received. With the right attitude, you can win people to your cause for both long-term and short-term efforts. As with so many of the Principles of Success, you'll discover that the practice of cooperation brings not only direct rewards, but many attendant benefits that will be useful in building your dreams.

THE TEXT

This is distinctly an age of cooperation in which we are living. The outstanding achievements in business, industry, finance, transportation and politics are all based upon the principle of cooperative effort.

You can hardly read a daily paper one week in succession without seeing notice of

---

[4] Dr. Hill used the spelling "co-operation," which was acepted at the time The Ladder to Success was published. To avoid distraction, we have chosen to use the contemporary spelling.

some consolidation or merger of business or industrial interests. These mergers and friendly alliances of business are based upon cooperation, because cooperation brings together in a spirit of harmony of purpose all the energies, whether human or mechanical, so that they function as one, without friction.

Without intending it, Dr. Hill is being prophetic. In the more than seventy years that have passed since he wrote these words, cooperation has become more important than ever. Mergers continue in the name of competitive advantage. When companies divest themselves of divisions, they spin off only those sectors which are not part of their core enterprises and therefore are unable to work cooperatively with the rest of the company. (An exception does occur when government intervenes to prevent monopolies in certain markets).

Government itself becomes ever more cooperative: international agencies abound, drawing on expertise from many countries and sharing the cost of mutual benefits. The first truly permanent space station will be the result of just this kind of cooperation. Around the world, professional and technical associations are legion. Tools such as the Internet provide an important advantage in sharing information and coordinating activity. And despite all this progress, there is no reason to believe that cooperation is anywhere near reaching its limits. Those of us who are alive seventy years from now will be amazed at what is being done cooperatively that was once attempted in only fragmented efforts.

The complexity of the modern world requires cooperation.

Knowledge grows ever more specialized, resources become ever more precious, and there are more and more issues that must be addressed as we come to understand the effects of human activity on the environment. Cooperation is the wave of the future.

And to succeed in the future–tomorrow as much as seventy years from now–you need to be able to inspire cooperation. You need it from co-workers, family members, neighbors, government officials, the media, and even from the mechanic at the humble gas station. Inspiring cooperation in others is an art, but like many arts, it rests on the technical skills that one might call craft. You have been learning this craft.

You will observe that some of the preceding Laws of this course must be practiced as a matter of habit before one can get perfect cooperation from others. For example, other people will not cooperate with you unless you have mastered and apply the Law of a *Pleasing Personality.* You will also notice that *Enthusiasm* and *Self-Control* and the *Habit of Doing More than Paid for* must be practiced before you can hope to gain full cooperation from others.

These Laws overlap one another, and all of them must be merged into the Law of *cooperation,* which means that one, to gain cooperation from others, must form the habit of practicing the Laws named.

No man is willing to cooperate with a person who has an offensive Personality. No man is willing to cooperate with one who is not

Enthusiastic, or who lacks Self-Control. *Power* comes from organized, cooperative effort!

It is worth noting here that PMA, a Positive Mental Attitude, is another significant asset in inspiring cooperation. PMA combines enthusiasm and self-control into aspects of a pleasing personality. Your can-do attitude comes across as a reasonable one, inspiring confidence in people who contemplate working with you. Opportunities for doing more than you are expected to do become easy to spot and you have no difficulty motivating yourself to engage in this extra effort because you know that your labor will bear fruit in time.

An Amazing Offer

Dr. Hill, always a practical man and eager to share his ideas, provides us with a very concrete demonstration of all the ways in which cooperation can be inspired.

A few years ago the president of a well-known real estate company addressed the following letter to the author:

DEAR MR. HILL:

Our firm will give you a check for $10,000.00 if you will show us how to get the confidence of the public as effectively as you do in connection with the work in which you are engaged.

Very cordially,

To this letter the following reply was sent:

DEAR MR. J–:

May I not thank you for the compliment, and

while I could use your check for $10,000.00, I am per-
fectly willing to give you, gratis, what information I have
on the subject. If I have unusual ability to gain cooperation from other people, it is because of the following
reasons:

1. I render more service than I ask people to
   pay for.
2. I engage in no transaction, intentionally,
   which does not benefit all whom it affects.
3. I make no statements which I do not believe
   to be true.
4. I have a sincere desire in my heart to be of
   useful service to the greatest number
   of people.
5. I like people better than I like money.
6. I am doing my best to *live* as well as to *teach*
   my own philosophy of success.
7. I accept no favors, from anyone, without giv
   ing favors in return.
8. I ask nothing of any person without having a
   right to that thing for which I ask.
9. I enter into no arguments with people over
   trivial matters.
10. I spread the sunshine of optimism and good
    cheer wherever and whenever I can.
11. I never flatter people for the purpose of gain
    ing their confidence.
12. I sell counsel and advice to other people, at
    a modest price, but *never offer free advice.*
13. While teaching others how to achieve suc
    cess, I have demonstrated that I can make
    my philosophy work for myself as well, thus

"practicing that which I preach."

14. I am so thoroughly sold on the work in which I am engaged that my enthusiasm over it becomes "contagious" and others are influenced by it.

If there are other elements entering into what you believe to be my ability to get the confidence of others, I do not know what they are. Incidentally, your letter raised an interesting question, and caused me to analyze myself as I had never done before. For this reason I refuse to accept your check, on the grounds that you have caused me to do something which may be worth many times ten thousand dollars.

Very cordially,

NAPOLEON HILL

Turn any of the statements in the above letter around and you will find some very fast ways to destroy your chances of cooperation. Would you cooperate with someone who could say of himself or herself, "I render less service than people pay for"? Or, "I have no desire to be of service to anyone"? Of course not. In cooperating, people take a risk. They may lose money, time, good will, even self-esteem if their work with you goes awry. There are no guarantees that any undertaking will succeed, but only the desperate or the foolish will cooperate with someone who they do not feel they can trust.

Michael Dell notes that when Dell Computers was a young company, he was able to persuade some very experienced business leaders to join the corporate board. This was a significant asset for Dell, because it allowed them to obtain financing and strike deals with established companies that depended on the confidence that these board members inspired. Of course, these board members were not simply lending their prestige to just anyone. They met Michael Dell, and he inspired their cooperation because he possessed all the attributes that you have been studying in this course.

The ability to inspire cooperation flows from your mastery of the other Principles of Success, as well as from the finer points that Dr. Hill notes above. If there is any Principle on which you need work–or any item in the above list that is not true of yourself–then begin today to make the changes that will allow you to inspire cooperation.

Lesson Fourteen
PROFITING BY FAILURE

SUMMARY

As you charge your mind with ideas of success, the prospect of failure is unpleasant. But everyone experiences defeats, some large, some small. What separates those who ultimately achieve their dreams from those who stumble and leave the race is the ability to learn important lessons from what Shakespeare called "the slings and arrows of outrageous fortune."

Though it may seem ironic for a philosophy of success to extol the significance of failure, Dr. Hill considered it an essential experience, one that could be built upon for the ultimate achievement of great things. What matters most when you suffer defeats is not the extent of your losses, but your ability to examine them and learn from what they teach you.

THE TEXT

A wealthy philosopher by the name of Croesus, was an official counselor to his majesty, King Cyrus. He said some very wise things, in his capacity as court philosopher, among them this:

'I am remindod, O king, and take this lesson to heart, that there is a wheel on which the affairs of men revolve, and its mechanism is such that it prevents *any* man from being *always* fortunate.'

It is true; there is a sort of unseen Fate, or wheel, turning in the lives of all of us, and sometimes it brings us good fortune and sometimes ill fortunes, despite anything that we as individual human beings, can do. However, this wheel obeys the law of averages, thereby insuring us against continuous ill fortune. If ill fortune comes today, there is hope in the thought that its opposite will come in the next turn of the wheel, or the one following the next, etc.

Failure is one of the most beneficial parts of a human being's experience, for the reason that there are many needed lessons that must be learned before one commences to succeed which could not be learned by any teacher other than *failure*.

Failure is always a blessing in disguise, providing it teaches us some useful lesson that we could not or would not have learned without it!

However, millions of people make the mistake of accepting *failure* as final, whereas it is, like most other events in life, but transitory and for this reason should not be accepted as final.

The message of the last three paragraphs can be difficult to accept when you are contemplating the loss of money and effort because of something you did not anticipate. Yet even as he wrote these words, Dr. Hill was experiencing defeat himself.

Why this Book was once a Failure

His landmark book, *The Law of Success*, had been published just two years before, in 1928. Strong initial sales grew into even better sales, and the book was a national bestseller. But in October, 1929, the collapse of the stock market soured the minds of most Americans on the idea that success was the result of their own efforts. The Great Depression took money out of their pockets, and Dr. Hill saw sales of his book plummet.

Nothing Dr. Hill could have done would have prevented the Great Depression. Twenty years' of work had gone into *The Law of Success*, and the financial security it could have provided him vanished. It was a devastating blow. Yet, you hold in your hands a demonstration that Dr. Hill moved quickly to adjust to his losses by producing a less expensive, single volume that brought the same message to the public at a much smaller cost.

Unfortunately, it did not work.

Though well-regarded, *The Ladder to Success* did not address the greatest issue facing Dr. Hill's readers: their loss of belief in themselves and the economic system. Its sales were not enough to compensate for the income lost by the falloff in sales of *The Law of Success*. Like so many Americans in those years, Dr. Hill was forced into drastic economies, giving up his new home. He spent the next several years working on behalf of the new Roosevelt administration in an effort to buoy the mood of the country

The failure that he had twice experienced planted a seed in his mind. There had to be a different way to convey his message to people who wanted something more out of

life. Dr. Hill spent several more years gaining new experience of the way in which people succeeded and failed, and
at last he felt himself ready to write a new book. In 1937,
he released *Think and Grow Rich.* The book was an instant
classic that continues as an essential guide to achievement
today.

The Principles of Success had already been defined
ten years before, but it was only through the wrenching
defeats of the intervening decade that Dr. Hill gained the
wisdom necessary to present them in the format that revolutionized motivational writing. To an outside observer in the
early 1930s, it might have seemed that Napoleon Hill had
had his chance at the brass ring, and missed. But that
observer would have overlooked the importance of profiting
by failure. Dr. Hill did not.

No matter what happens to you, you are not truly
defeated unless you decide that you are.

Successful people must learn to distinguish between *failure* and *temporary defeat.*
Every person experiences, at one time or
another, some form of temporary defeat, and
out of such experiences come some of the
greatest and most beneficial lessons.

In truth, most of us are so constituted
that if we never experienced temporary defeat
(or what some ignorantly call *failure*), we would
soon become so egotistical and independent
that we would imagine ourselves more important than the Deity. There are few such people
in this world, and it is said of them that they
refer to Deity, if at all, as "*Me* and God," with a
heavy emphasis on the *"Me!"*

Headaches are beneficial, despite the fact that they are very disagreeable, for the very reason that they represent Nature's language in which she calls loudly for the intelligent use of the human body; particularly of the stomach and tributary organs through which most of us create the majority of physical human ills.

It is the same regarding Temporary Defeat or Failure–these are Nature's symbols through which she signals us that we have been headed in the wrong direction, and if we are reasonably intelligent we heed these signals, steer a different course, and come, finally, to the objective of our *definite chief aim.*

Again we see that a little success can be a dangerous thing. Succeed at a few things and it becomes impossible to imagine that you will not always succeed at everything. Arrogance creeps into your actions. Accurate Thinking may suffer, along with aspects of a Pleasing Personality. Self-control seems unnecessary, because, after all, the self seems to be doing very well.

And this is how people come to experience failure that is not the result of fortune, but of their own error. These kinds of failure are even more instructive, as they show you flaws in your own thinking that must be corrected. The lesson that must be learned in these cases, however, is not that you are incapable of success, but that you must still adjust your thoughts and actions to achieve it. Though it is painful to be brought up short by your own mistakes, it is unavoidable, and the best response is not to lament your error, but to begin working immediately to correct it. This willingness to engage in self-examination is essential.

The author of this philosophy has devoted more than a quarter of a century to research for the purpose of discovering what characteristics were possessed and employed by the successful men and women in the field of business, industry, politics, statesmanship, religion, finance, transportation, science, etc. This research has involved the reading of more than one thousand books of a scientific, business, and biographical nature, or an average of more than one such book a week.

One of the most startling discoveries made by this enormous amount of research was the fact that all the outstanding successes, regardless of the field of endeavor in which they were engaged, were people who met with reverses, adversity, temporary defeat, and in some instances, actual *permanent failure* (as far as they, as individuals, were concerned). Not one single successful person was discovered whose success was attained without the experience of what, in many instances, seemed like unbearable obstacles that had to be mastered.

It was discovered also *that in exact ratio to the extent that these successful people met squarely and did not budge from defeat they arose to the heights of success.* In other words, success is measured, always, by the extent to which an individual meets and

squarely deals with the obstacles that arise in
the course of his procedure in pursuit of his
definite chief aim.

Dr. Hill next provides a long list of great successes
who suffered stinging defeats: Columbus, Edison,
Alexander Graham Bell, Woolworth, Robert Fulton, the
Wright Brothers, and Henry Ford. To them we could add
many modern examples, including every politician in office
today, along with Bill Gates (remember the software called
"Bob?") and just about every other person cited in this book.

Defeat is not the end. It is a chance to begin anew,
wiser than you were before and enriched by the knowledge
that there is no blow this side of death from which you cannot recover. Face your setbacks with certainty that there is a
lesson to be learned and you will learn it and build from
your mistakes a stronger, more satisfying plan for making
yourself a success.

Lesson Fifteen
TOLERANCE

SUMMARY

An intolerant person lives in a single world, defined by an unbreakable set of rules and a nearby horizon. The tolerant person lives in a world of endless possibilities, where all limits are open to challenge and any barrier can be overcome. Which of these people stands a greater chance of achieving something great?

Tolerance is much more than simply an aspect of social justice, practiced as a courtesy to others. It is a principle that liberates *you* as much as your neighbor. It offers you the opportunity to become wise, adaptive, and intellectually curious. It also frees you from many sources of trouble and distraction. It is the inevitable expression of many of the preceding lessons, and it must be embraced fully in order to advance to the final two Principles of Success.

THE TEXT

Dr. Hill's message here is characteristically straightforward. It will also seem astoundingly apt for the early twenty-first century.

Intolerance has caused more grief than any other of man's many forms of ignorance. Practically all wars grow out of intolerance. Misunderstandings between "capital" and "labor" are usually the outgrowth of intolerance.

It is impossible for any man to observe the Law on *Accurate Thought*, without having first acquired the habit of tolerance, for the reason that intolerance causes a man to fold the Book of Knowledge and write, "Finis, I know it all!" on the cover.

The most damaging form of intolerance grows out of religious and racial differences of opinion. Civilization, as we know it today, bears the deep wounds of gross intolerance all back down the ages, mostly those of a religious nature.

This is the most democratic country on earth. We are the most cosmopolitan people on earth. We are made up of all nationalities and people of every religious belief. We live side by side with neighbors whose religion differs from our own. Whether we are good neighbors or bad depends largely on how tolerant we are with one another.

Intolerance is the result of ignorance, or stated conversely, the lack of *knowledge.* Well-informed men are seldom intolerant, because they know that no man knows enough to entitle him to judge others by his standards.

Through the principle of social heredity we inherit, from our environment, and through our early religious teachings, our ideas of religion. Our teachers themselves may not always be right, and if we bear this thought in mind, we would not allow such teachings to influence us to believe that we have a corner on *truth,* and that people whose teachings on this subject have been different from our own are all wrong.

There are many reasons why one should be tolerant, the chief of them being the fact that tolerance permits cool reason to guide one in the direction of *facts,* and this, in turn, leads to *accurate thinking.*

It may not be your *duty* to be tolerant with other people whose ideas, religious views, politics, and racial tendencies are different from yours, but it is *your privilege!* You do not have to ask permission of anyone to be tolerant because this is something you control in your own mind; therefore, the responsibility that goes with the choice is also your own.

Intolerance is closely related to the *six basic fears* described in the Law of Self-Confidence, and it may be stated as a positive fact that intolerance is always the result of *fear* or *ignorance.* There are no exceptions to this rule. The moment another person (providing he, himself, is not intolerant) discovers that you are cursed with intolerance, he can easily and quickly mark you as either the victim of *fear* and *superstition* or what is worse, *ignorance.*

Intolerance closes the doorway to opportunity in a thousand ways, and shuts out the light of intelligence.

The moment you open your mind to *facts,* and take the attitude that the last word is seldom said on any subject–that there always remains the chance that still more truth may be learned on every subject, you begin to cultivate the Law of *Tolerance*, and if you practice this habit for long you will soon become a thinker, with ability to solve the problems that confront you in your struggle to make a place for yourself in your chosen field of endeavor.

This is such a direct and powerful statement on the importance of tolerance that it is impossible to provide any substantial elaboration on the reasons why this Principle is essential to your efforts to achieve your definite chief aim.

Instead, let us look for a moment at the ways that intolerance can creep into your thinking.

The Intolerance Test

Do you:

1) Discount ideas and suggestions because of what you think you know about the person who offers them?
2) Avoid people whose ideas or ways of living are contrary to your own?
3) Seek out opinions that only agree with yours?
4) Devote time and energy to making your work place or neighborhood inhospitable to people who are not like you?
5) Tell stories or jokes that depend on stereotypical assumptions about someone's character, or intelligence?
6) Never read books except those which are

immediately practical?
7) Feel that there is a right and wrong side of
   every issue?
8) Consider yourself an irrefutable expert on
   any subject?
9) Expect unswerving agreement from people
   who are subordinate to you?
10) Feel you haven't ever learned anything
    more important than the ideas you grew up with?

No one wants to think he or she is intolerant. The dangers of that mindset are obvious. But since thoughts are habits, we all run the risk of reinforcing intolerant aspects of our thinking simply by repeating them again and again without realizing what they imply. When we are fortunate enough to live in a tolerant society, the danger is that no one will challenge our small mistakes until they grow into something ugly or cause a significant problem.

You want to weed out intolerant habits before they cause harm to others and to you. It is always a good idea to examine regularly all your convictions. This practice is not done out of uncertainty, but out of a desire to be accurate. Such examinations may reveal all kinds of small errors that have blinded you to opportunities or left you open to setbacks. While learning from defeat is important, so is learning to prevent defeat based on inaccurate opinions and ideas.

No one who reads Dr. Hill's essay on tolerance can fail to be struck by just how pertinent it is to the issues which trouble the world at the start of the twenty-first century. In this he was, sadly, not a prophet, but a student of human nature who recognized how some of the oldest of human failings retain their power to inflict grief and misery no matter how far our knowledge and science have progressed.

It may not be possible for you to directly impact a climate of global intolerance, but that worldwide climate is created by thousands of local climates, to which each of us contributes. Simply by embracing tolerance for its effect on your own ambitions, you can play a part in shifting the balance of tolerance throughout the world. In doing so, you amplify your opportunities to achieve things that might never be possible in a world where every person is certain he knows all there is to say about truth.

Lesson Sixteen
PRACTICING THE GOLDEN RULE

SUMMARY

Here, all the other Principles of Success are distilled. Though the Golden Rule may seem to be merely a platitude that weary parents use to scold their children, it is, in truth, the manifestation of an enduring universal function that has a powerful impact on your efforts to achieve success.

As a kind of mantra, the Golden Rule will guide your decision-making. It will also repay your choices with consequences that are perfectly in line with the nature of the decisions you make. It's easy to see just how this Principle will affect you; what requires effort is the conscious dedication to making the most of its power.

THE TEXT

This is, in many ways, the most important of the Seventeen Laws of Success.

Despite the fact that the great philosophers of more than five thousand years have all discovered the Law of the Golden Rule, and have made comment on it, the great majority of people of today look upon it as a sort of pretty text for preachers to build sermons on.

In truth, the Golden Rule philosophy is based upon a powerful law which, when understood and faithfully practiced, will enable any man to get others to cooperate with him.

It is a well-known truth that most men follow the practice of returning good or evil, act for act. If you slander a man, he will slander you in return. If you praise a man, he will praise you in return. If you favor a man in business, he will favor you in return.

There are exceptions to this rule, to be sure, but by and large the law works out. Like attracts like. This is in accordance with a great natural law, and it works in every particle of matter and in every form of energy in the universe. Successful men attract successful men. Failures attract failures. The professional "bum" will make a bee line for the "flop" house, where he may associate with other "bums," even though he may be set down in a strange city, after dark.

The law of the Golden Rule is closely related to the Law on *The Habit of Doing More than Paid for.* The very act of rendering more service than you are paid to render puts into operation this law through which "like attracts like," which is the selfsame law as that which forms the basis of the Golden Rule philosophy.

To understand how important the Law of the Golden Rule is, consider your life, not as a series of separate actions, but as a sum total of all your actions. There will be strong and weak points, errors in judgment, and some anomalous choices. But the quality of your thoughts and decisions is exactly what you should expect to receive, in turn, from the rest of the world.

If your efforts are shoddy, your intentions deceitful, and your mood pessimistic, you will find that the world provides you with experiences of the same kind. If your work is passable, your intentions ambiguous, and your mood inconstant, you will find that life offers you the same. If you desire excellence, honesty and optimism, therefore, you can only find them by creating them in yourself.

"Do unto others as you would have others do unto you," says the Golden Rule. An important codicil should be, "Think about others as you would have others think about you." Thoughts, as much as actions, come under the Golden Rule. Fill your mind with criticism, and you inspire it elsewhere. Contemplate dishonesty, and you can expect to be served from the same dish.

The thoughts that dominate your mind direct your actions. Sometimes this effect of obvious, but it is often subtle and not immediately discernable. Yet this is why bad faith efforts are repaid with even more bad faith, and good faith efforts return unexpected benefits.

The Human Mystery

This law is so fundamental, so obvious, yet so simple. It is one of the great mysteries of human nature that it is not generally understood and practiced. Back of its use lie possibilities that stagger the imagination of the most visionary person. Through its use one may learn the real secret–all the secret there is–about the art of *getting others to do that which we wish them to do.*

If you want a favor from someone,

make it your business to seek out the person
from whom you want the favor and, in an
appropriate moment, render that person an
equivalent of the favor you wish from him. If
he does not respond at first, double the dose
and render him another favor, and another,
and another, and so on, until finally he will, out
of shame if nothing more, some back and render you a favor.

*You get others to cooperate with you by
first cooperating with them!*

The foregoing sentence is worth reading
a hundred times, for it contains the gist of one
of the most powerful laws available to the man
who has the intention of attaining great success.

It may sometimes happen, and it will,
that the particular person to whom you render
useful service will never respond and render
you a similar service, but *keep this important
truth in mind*–that even though one person fails
to respond, someone else will observe the
transaction and, out of a sportsman's desire to
see justice done, or perhaps with a more self-
ish motive in mind, will render you the service
to which you are entitles.

'Whatsoever a man soweth that shall he
also reap!'

This is more than a preachment; it is a
great practical truth that may be made the
foundation of every successful achievement.
From winding pathways or straight, every

thought you send out, every deed you perform, will gather a flock of other thoughts or deeds according to its own nature, and come back home to you in due time.

There is no escape from this truth. It is as eternal as the universe, as sure of operation as the law of gravitation. To ignore it is to mark yourself as ignorant, or indifferent, either of which will destroy your chances of success.

But to embrace the truth of the Golden Rule is to consolidate all your actions toward the pursuit of your definite chief aim. All the effort and energy you expend to make yourself effective, courageous, hard-working, and cooperative will return to you amplified. The work you do beyond what is expected of you, the enthusiasm you show, the imagination you cultivate, the positive mental attitude that you create will influence what life gives you.

The Golden Rule is not an insurance policy. It does not prevent any single action that might be harmful to you. But it does determine the balance of what life offers you. By determining what you offer the world in exchange for the success you desire, you also determine the nature of what the world will use to repay you.

Knowing this, you can make any decision on the basis of the Golden Rule. You may choose short-term advantage over long-term benefit, if that is what you want from life. You may choose to get by rather than to excel, if that is what you want from life. You can choose dishonesty, intolerance, or a host of other qualities in your actions, *if that is what you want from life.*

What do you want from life?

149

Lesson Seventeen
THE HABIT OF HEALTH

SUMMARY

Personal health may seem an unusual element to include in the Principles of Success, but it is a part of nearly everyone's definition of success, if simply at a subconscious level. Maintaining good health is not simply a matter of allowing yourself to be able to enjoy the fruits of your labors. It is essential to be able to devote the maximum mental and physical energy to what you set out to do.

Ideas about creating and maintaining good physical health have changed since Dr. Hill's days, but his emphasis on mental health was ahead of its time, as so much of his thinking was.

THE TEXT

We come now to the last of the seventeen factors of success. In previous chapters we have learned that success grows out of *power*, and that power is organized knowledge expressed in definite *action*. No one can remain intensely active for long without good health. The mind will not function properly unless it has a sound body in which to function. Practically all of the other sixteen factors which enter into the building of success depend, for their successful application, upon a healthy body.

Good health is dependent, in the main, upon:

1. Proper food and air combinations;
2. Proper elimination of waste fecal matter
3. Proper exercise
4. Right thinking

It is not the purpose of this chapter to present a treatise on how to remain healthy, as that is a task which belongs to specialists in physical and mental therapeutics.... No one should experiment with fasting, dieting, or any other form of self-administered therapeutics, except under the direction of a physician of experience in such matters.

So just what is Dr. Hill telling us here?

Simply, diet, exercise and mental health all have a role to play in our ability to create success, and accordingly, we should not make the mistake of stinting any of them. It is very easy to slip into habits which seem to emphasize hard work–skipping meals, eating fast food all the time, spending hours at the desk–for the sake of productivity. But an improper emphasis on today's work over tomorrow's health is, in the long run, highly unproductive.

Item four in the above list, Right Thinking, is of particular importance in creating and maintaining good mental and physical health. Callers to the Napoleon Hill Foundation for many years were greeted by Executive Director Michael J. Ritt. When asked how he was doing, Ritt's response was an enthusiastic "I'm happy, healthy and terrific!" It has been a self-fulfilling prophecy.

The alternative course is to worry, or to avoid thinking about your health altogether, and both of these are mistakes. Worry tends to create more mental and physical problems, from a queasy stomach to skin disorders or worse. Ignoring a potential problem prevents necessary diagnosis and treatment. Keep your mental state positive, but remain alert to changes in your body or your spirits. Seek professional help as necessary, and adhere to the recommendations given to you. The sooner you begin addressing what is wrong, the sooner you will correct the problem and be restored to your old self.

Good health is created and maintained through the proper frame of mind. Dr. Hill was not a pioneer in this regard; he was simply an astute observer of human beings. If you want to find out more on this topic, there are many worthy books to investigate, including those of Norman Cousins, and Deepak Chopra.

Keep in mind, though, that not all ill-health is caused by negative thinking. While we can increase our resistance to bacteria and viruses through PMA, we do not make ourselves immune. Disease has been with human beings since the beginning, and our bodies are not meant to last forever. Do not make the mistake of assuming that because you do become ill, you are at fault. It's far better to concentrate on getting well as soon as possible than to beat yourself up because you don't feel well.

The PMA you devote to maintaining good health is another of the wonderfully self-reinforcing effects that comes with living by the Principles of Success. The more attention you pay to thinking—and acting—as a healthy person, the healthier you are in the long run.

Good health allows you to create success, and even more importantly, allows you to enjoy it.

THE THIRTY MOST COMMON CAUSES
OF FAILURE

SUMMARY

At first, it seems that Dr. Hill has merely added a few appendices to *The Ladder of Success*. In New Orleans, this might be called a *lagniappe*, or a little something extra that a merchant offers a customer along with a purchase. But what follows the lessons on the Principles of Success is more than the extra roll that makes up a baker's dozen.

In the following chapters, he writes forcefully of the power of his ideas and gives highly practical suggestions for implementing them. His vision of the potential of the Principles of Success is dramatic and accurate, as we shall see.

He begins with a crisp reminder of the ways in which people can undermine their efforts to achieve their ambitions. Run through this checklist and see if any of these thirty items are holding you back. The preceding Principles of Success have given you the skills and tools necessary to correct anything which might be hindering your progress toward success. It may not be pleasant to think that you are sabotaging yourself this way, but it is far more pleasant to enjoy the attainment of your definite chief aim.

THE TEXT

Through the foregoing pages you have had a brief description of the seventeen factors through which success is attained. Now let us turn our attention to some of the factors which cause failure. Check the list and you will perhaps find here the cause of any failure, or temporary defeat, which you may have experienced. The list is based on accurate analysis of over twenty thousand failures, and it covers men and women in every calling.

1. *Unfavorable hereditary foundation.* (This cause of failure stands at the head of the list. Bad breeding is a handicap against which there is but little remedy, and it is one for which the individual, unfortunately, is not responsible.)

At first glance, Dr. Hill seems to be suggesting that bad genes hold some people back. But it is important to recognize that he regarded heredity as a social construct as much as a genetic one. People who come from environments in which achievement is denigrated, along with the skills necessary for it, will always be struggling to overcome limitations of belief. Most significantly, they are under the mistaken impression that success is due to chance or that people of their backgrounds are incapable of it. They do not become successes because they do not believe they can try. There is, indeed little remedy for this attitude, unless, on a case by case basis, people who are handicapped in this way are given reason to question their social heredity.

Part of the mission of the Napoleon Hill Foundation has been to provide an education in the idea of success to people who believe they cannot succeed. Through educational programs in the nation's prisons, the Foundation seeks to inspire ambition in men and women whose environments taught them that they were not good enough for success.

2. Lack of a well-defined purpose, or definite aim toward which to strive.
3. Lack of ambition to aim above mediocrity.
4. Insufficient education.
5. Lack of self-discipline and tact, generally manifesting itself through all sorts of excesses; especially sexual desire and eating
6. Ill-health, usually due to preventable causes
7. Unfavorable environment during childhood, when character was being formed, resulting in vicious habits of body and mind

While this might seem to be a repetition of the first cause, people who stumble for this reason do not lack belief in the idea of attainable success; they simply feel that there is nothing wrong with achieving success by any means necessary

8. Procrastination
9. Lack of persistence and courage to blame one's self with one's failures

The most obvious manifestation of this is the refusal to learn from defeat.

10. Negative personality
11. Lack of a well-defined sexual urge
12. An uncontrollable desire to get something for nothing usually manifesting itself in habits of gambling
13. Lack of decision
14. One or more of the six basic fears described

elsewhere in this book
15. Poor selection of a mate in marriage
16. Overcaution, destroying initiative and self-confidence
17. Poor selection of associates in business
18. Superstition and prejudice, generally trace able to a lack of knowledge of natural laws
19. Wrong selection of occupation
20. Dissipation of energies, through lack of understanding of the law of concentration.
21. Lack of thrift
22. Lack of enthusiasm
23. Intolerance
24. Intemperance in eating, drinking, and sexual activities
25. Inability to cooperate with others in a spirit of harmony
26. Possession of power which was not acquired through self-effort, by slow evolutionary processes of experience (as in the case of one who inherits wealth or is placed in a position of power to which he is not entitled by merit.
27. Dishonesty
28. Egotism and vanity
29. Guessing instead of thinking
30. Lack of capital

Some may wonder why "lack of capital" was placed at the bottom of the list, and the answer is that anyone who can qualify with a reasonably high grade, on the other twenty-nine causes of failure, can always get all the capital needed for any purpose whatsoever.

The foregoing list does not include all the causes of failure but it does represent the most common causes. Some may object that "unfavorable luck" should have been added to the list, but the answer to that complaint is that luck, or the law of chance, is subject to mastery by all who understand how to apply the seventeen factors of success. However, in fairness to those who may never have had the opportunity to master the seventeen factors, it must be admitted that luck, or an unfavorable turn of the wheel of chance, is sometimes the cause of failure.

Those who are inclined to attribute all their failures to "circumstances" or luck should remember the blunt injunction laid down by Napoleon, who said, "To hell with circumstances! I create circumstances." Most "circumstances" and unfavorable results of luck are self-made also. *Let us not forget this!*

This is Dr. Hill's philosophy in a nutshell. For better or worse, we create the lives we lead. Successful people are those who acknowledge this, and act accordingly.

Here is a statement of fact, and a confession, that is well-worth remembering. *The law of success philosophy, which is now rendering useful service to men and woman all over this earth, is very largely the result of nearly twenty years of so-called failure upon the part of the author.* In the more extensive course on the Law of Success philosophy, under the lesson on "Profiting by Failure", the student will observe that the author met with failure and adversity and reverses so often that he might have been justified in crying out, "Luck is against me!" Seven major failures, and more scores of minor failures than the author cares to remember, laid the foundation for a philosophy which is now bringing success to tens of thousands of people, *including the author!* "Bad luck" has been harnessed and put to work...

"There is a wheel on which the affairs of men revolve, and its mechanism is such that it prevents any man from being always fortunate."

True enough! There is a such a wheel of life, but it is rotating continuously. If this wheel brings misfortune today, it can be made to bring good fortune tomorrow. If this were not true, the Law of Success philosophy would be a farce and a fake, offering nothing but false hope.

The author was once told that he would always be a failure because he was born under an unfavorable star! Something must have happened to antidote the bad influence of that star, and something *has happened.* That something is the power to master obstacles by first mastering self, which grew out of understanding and application of the Law of Success philosophy. If the seventeen factors of success can offset the bad influence of a star for this author, they can do the same for *you*, or for any other person.

Laying our misfortunes to the influence of stars is just another way of acknowledging our ignorance or our laziness. The only place that stars can bring you bad luck is in your own mind. You have possession of that mind, and it has the power to master all the bad influences which stand between you and success, including that of the stars.

If you really wish to see the cause of your bad luck and misfortune, do not look up toward the stars; look in a mirror. You are the master of your fate! You are the captain of your soul...You have a mind which you, alone, control, and this mind can be stimulated and made to form a direct contact with all the power you need to solve any problem that may confront you. The person who blames his troubles upon stars thereby challenges the existence of Infinite Intelligence, or God, if you prefer that name.

It should come as little surprise that Dr. Hill is dismissive of the notion that our fates are dictated by something other than human choice. "What the mind can conceive and believe, the mind can achieve," is a philosophy that leaves little room for ascribing personal achievement to arcane influences. Yet you do not need to follow astrology in order to make similar erroneous assumptions.

When you sat down to write out your definite chief

aim, did you shy away from your true goal in order to come up with something that seemed "reasonable" or "doable"? Were you accepting limitations that other people have told you about, just as someone once told Dr. Hill that he was star-crossed? What would have happened if he had accepted that notion? What will happen to you if you do not accept someone else's limits?

Whatever you lack in your life, you lack because you have not yet pursued it. If you have begun pursuit, the thing will be yours. But if you never pursue it, you will always feel the lack of the thing that *you decided* you could not have.

The Mystery of the Power of Thought

In front of the author's study, at Broadway and Forty-fourth Street in New York City, stands the Paramount Building; a great, tall, impressive building which serves as a daily reminder of the great power of *thought.*

Come, stand with me by the window of my study and let us analyze this modern skyscraper. Tell me, if you can, of what materials the building is constructed. Immediately you will say, "Why is it built of brick and steel girders and plate glass and lumber," and you will be partly right, but you have not told the entire story.

The brick and steel and other materials which went into the *physical* portion of the building were necessary, but before any of those materials were laid into place the building, in its entirety, was constructed of another sort of material. It was built, in the mind of Adolph Zukor, out of the intangible stuff known as *thought*.

Everything you have or ever will have, good or bad, was attracted to you by the nature of your *thoughts*. Positive thoughts attract positive, desirable objects; negative thoughts attract poverty and misery and a flock of other sorts of undesirable objects. Your brain is the magnet to which everything you possess clings, and make no mistake about this, your brain will not attract success while you are thinking of poverty and failure.

Every man is where he is, as the result of his own dominating thoughts, just as surely as night follows day. *Thought* is the only thing that you absolutely control, a statement of fact which we repeat because of its great significance. You do not control, entirely, the money you possess, or the love and friendship that you enjoy; you had nothing to do with your coming into the world and you will have but little to do with the time of your going; but you do have *everything* to do with the state of your own mind. You can make that mind *positive* or you can permit it to become negative, as the result of outside influences and suggestions. Divine Providence gave you supreme control of your own mind, and with this control the responsibility that is now yours to make the best use of it.

In your own mind you can fashion a great building, similar to the one which stands in front of the author's study, and then transform that mental picture into a reality, just as Adolph Zukor did, because the material out of which he constructed the Paramount Building is available to every human beings; moreover, it is *free*.

The difference between success and failure is largely a matter of the difference between positive and negative thought. A negative mind will not attract a fortune. Like attracts like. Nothing attracts success as quickly as success. Poverty begets more poverty. Become successful and the whole world will lay its treasure at your feet and want to do something to help you become more successful. Show signs of poverty and the entire world will try to take away that which you have of value. You can borrow money at the bank when you are prosperous and do not need it, but try and arrange a loan when you are poverty-stricken, or when some great emergency threatens you. You are the master of your own destiny because you control the one thing which can change and redirect the course of human destinies, the power of thought. Let this great truth sink into your consciousness and this book will have marked the most important turning point of your life.

The Paramount Building no longer towers over

Broadway. In the turbulent world of Manhattan real estate, Adolph Zukor's ambitious project has been replaced by other skyscrapers as a part of the renewal of Times Square. But Dr. Hill's point remains the same: every great achievement begins in the human mind. Glass, steel and brick are useless without a guiding vision of what they can become; such visions arise only through the thoughts of those who dare to imagine they can change the world around them.

The power of your thoughts is the single most effective tool you have in achieving success. It is, in truth, the only tool, for no matter what else you use to create what you desire in life, it is the nature of your thoughts that determines what, if anything, happens. Simply accepting this idea will fundamentally alter your approach to life, as you become conscious of the positive or negative nature of your thinking.

When negative thinking creeps in, replace it immediately with positive thinking. Use PMA to reverse old habits of negativity. Reverse the polarity of a negative mind, and a positive mind will show you how to change anything about your life that you do not like. But remember, positive thinking only reaches its fullest potential when it is expressed through positive action. Your mind is not truly positively charged until your thoughts are made real through the choices you make.

FORTY UNIQUE IDEAS FOR MAKING MONEY

Summary

The ideas that follow came, Dr. Hill says, through a consultation with a student who called on him. Using the Master Mind principle, they brainstormed and produced this remarkable list in a short time.

Several points stand out for today's reader. First, many of the ideas suggest developments that have taken place since *The Ladder of Success* was written. Second, most of those that have not been implemented still represent good opportunities for someone with the right inclinations. This list is not here to suggest what you should choose as your definite chief aim, but to underscore the usefulness of the kind of thinking that a Master Mind creates.

Some of these ideas seem to be close to what actually developed, but are missing an essential element. This is not surprising when one remembers that Dr. Hill and his partner were working spontaneously, while the people who did bring these ideas to the market devoted much careful study to their expression. Those who profited this way were applying many of the Principles of Success, such as Imagination and Accurate Thinking, and Dr. Hill would in no way be surprised to see just how useful those ideas had been in fulfilling the suggestions he makes below.

Text

1. Rewrite the Law of Success philoso-

phy in a brief form which can be presented in one volume, at a very low cost, so it can be placed in the hands of hundreds of students who might otherwise never have the benefit of such a philosophy of success, and permit teachers of the philosophy, throughout the world, to use this book as a textbook, in private classes and success clubs to be organized by them. (Author's note: The book you hold in your hands is the concrete result of the foregoing idea.)

2. A chain of automatic gas filling stations at which the motorist may serve himself, day or night, by dropping coins in a slot machine.

The self-serve gas station is a very tidy expression of this idea. Though it is wonderful to contemplate gas prices that would allow us to fill our tanks with a few coins, pay-at-the-pump is now commonplace for users of credit and debit cards.

3. A chain of automatic news stands, dispensing magazines, newspapers and periodicals through slot machines.

While there are few, if any, newsstands that operate this way, coin-operated vending machines for newspapers and magazines have been common for decades.

4. A chain of automatic five and ten cent stores, dispensing merchandise through slot machines, thus saving labor and loss from stealage over the counters.

No one, it seems, ever tried this idea, and modern

prices make it impossible now. But Philadelphia and New York both saw the development of the Automat, in which customers used coins to purchase food from banks of small, refrigerated compartments.

5. An elastic support, to be made of flexible steel, which will cause one to hold the spine and shoulders erect...

No one has yet created a comfortable device for ensuring good posture.

6. A vibrating machine, to be attached to the seats of chairs of office and factory workers who must work in a sitting position, which may be turned on at intervals during working hours, for the purpose of distributing the nervous energy and preventing fatigue.

A new word, "ergonomics," has been created to describe chairs and other equipment that are designed to prevent fatigue. The use of vibration as a tool for fatigue prevention seems to have been replaced, however, by its use for relaxation.

7. New profession of Environment Artist, whose work will be that of creating a positive environment in home, office, workshop, store, etc., for the purpose of relieving the monotony of such places.

There are, of course, many different types of specialists who design workplaces, homes and other environments according to various needs. Some are purely aesthetic, while others are created using principles of efficiency or, in the case of feng shui, ancient principles of natural harmony.

8. Combination locks for automobiles (keyless locks) for the prevention of theft, joy riding, etc.

Keyless locks are now common on car doors, and automotive engineers are developing them for ignition systems.

9. A new profession to be known as "Personality Artists," whose members will assist men and women in the selection of clothes of appropriate line and color harmony, to work in conjunction with high-grade clothing stores, and whose services will be free to the customer.

We now call these people "personal shoppers."

10. Research Secretary, whose business it will be to gather and classify data on any subject.

There are indeed, many people who provide these services, largely on a freelance basis, to writers, lawyers, historians, and anyone else with a need.

11. Country Club for people of small means, equipped with playgrounds for children, and competent nurses and play directors who will assume full responsibility for children during certain hours of the day or night, to be conducted in connection with suburban real estate developments, as an added inducement for people to locate there.

Child care centers are everywhere now, addressing the need that Dr. Hill identified here, even if they are rarely set up by real estate developers.

12. Idea Specialist for daily newspapers whose

business it would be to create new and unique ideas for sales and advertising campaigns for small merchants who cannot afford to employ expensive people, and whose services would be free to all advertisers of the paper.

Many papers now create special advertising promotions, such as one that features merchants in a particular area or who sell a particular type of merchandise. Large magazines have people dedicated to helping advertisers create unique promotions through their publications.

13. A Summer Camp Ground, near the city, where people may secure a plot of ground large enough for a tent, or small portable buildings, and sufficient ground for a garden, on a rental basis within the means of the man of small income.

The increasing popularity of the automobile made many places of this kind popular in the Northeast, though they tended to be rented for shorter periods of time. Cabins were much more common than tents, and gardens were rare, but Dr. Hill obviously recognized the need for escape from hot cities for country air.

14. Week-end outing information, supplying data on all near-by places of interest where the motorists may spend a day or a week-end's outing, with road maps, descriptive literature, etc., to be operated by chain of filling stations as a means of building up their business.

Maps, at least, became common promotional items for gas stations over the coming decades. Today, there are a number of books, targeted to specific areas, which provide suggested weekend getaway ideas, including maps, as well as dining and lodging information.

15. A moving picture service operated for the purpose of making short reels of children at play (to preserve the memory of their childhood days for parents), birthday parties, weddings, business gatherings, and banquets.

While technological advances have made it possible for many people to do these things themselves on an everyday basis, rarely are weddings without a hired photographer and videographer.

16. Typewriters for rent in hotels and on Pullman cars, though the aid of coin slot machines.

This idea has been expressed in several ways. At places such as Kinko's, where one may rent a computer or purchase the services of any of the other printing technologies that have replaced the typewriter, and at Internet cafes, one can also purchase computer time.

17. Box lunches for office and factory workers, made up of home-cooked foods, consisting of a properly balanced diet of pure food products. (Business can be conducted by a housewife, from her own kitchen). Several clients of the author are now profitably employing this idea.

In major urban areas, home cooks are usually supplanted nowadays by catering companies that provide these services to many offices, offering freshly prepared lunch in place of bags of chips and packaged cookies.

18. Home baking of pies, bread, and cakes, selling the output through regular arrangement with a number of local grocers and drug stores.

Home cooks have extended the range of products to include candy, cookies, salsa, preserves, baby food, and just about anything else for which they have a talent. They also sell to restaurants which want to advertise "home-made" desserts.

19. Book giving accurate information to beginners in the field of writing, as to subjects on which to write, and where and how to market their manuscripts.

At least one company, Writer's Digest Books, is now dedicated to providing this kind of information and any bookstore contains evidence of the usefulness of this idea.

20. Summer house boat that can be propelled by an automobile, for rent to motorists who wish to spend a part of their time on water and at the same time have their cars available for land use.

The need that Dr. Hill identifies here has been addressed in several ways, largely by the development of trailers for boats and the increasing addition of amenities to the boats themselves.

21. Window card advertising service for retail stores, carrying snappy, interesting epigrams instead of news pictures, that will cause the crowd to stop and read.

Businesses do not seem to have embraced this idea. People often drive by a place rather than walk nowadays, and roadside signs with changeable messages have replaced window cards in most places.

22. A set of fifty-two blotters, to be used for advertising purposes, each blotter carrying an epigram or motto appropriate to the business of the advertiser using the blotter, one blotter to be mailed out to a selected mailing list each week. (This is a plan to enable a printer to build up a business on printed blotters.)

The desk blotter is essentially a thing of the past. Perhaps something else might accomplish the same thing today.

23. Fountain drinks made of the juices of vegetables, which have food value, and served fresh each day, without preservatives or chemical of any sort.

Juice bars serving vegetable elixirs are everywhere now, from gyms and shopping malls to airports and grocery stores.

24. Signs for office doors made of removable glass, which may be taken along when a tenant moves.

The glass paneled office door now seems familiar to us only from vintage movies, but movable signs, particularly on a magnetic backing, follow businesses from location to location.

25. A Clearings House for the exchange of practical sales ideas among retailers.

This function has largely been taken up by trade

magazines.

26. A home nursery, to be conducted by married women, who wish an independent source of income, to serve women who wish to leave their children in reliable hands.

As noted before, child care centers are ubiquitous now.

27. Clothing Exchange, where used clothes may be exchanged for other used clothes.

While second-hand clothing stores are now common enough, no one has been able to make the idea of an exchange work, except on a charitable basis requiring subsidy.

28. New York City mailing address for out of the city small firms and individuals who wish their mail sent to New York and then forwarded, because of the prestige of the New York address, on a service fee of five dollars a month for each client. (Two hundred such client would give one person a very substantial income.)

Mail forwarding services now exist in every city in the country, providing a stable address for anyone who needs it. (Obviously, five dollars would no longer be a sufficient fee.)

29. Moving pictures for children for children only, catering exclusively to the child mind, based upon plots which educate as well as entertain, to be distributed through the public schools.

In an age when there is no shortage of media devoted to children, it can be hard to remember that in the early days of the movie industry, films were geared entirely to adults, and so the first part of Dr. Hill's idea is more forward-looking than it might appear. Educational movies and videos are now in frequent use in schools; some of them do manage to be entertaining as well.

30. Comic strip for newspapers, advertising some brand of merchandise, and at the same time entertaining, to be run in local newspapers by merchants selling the product advertised.

The closest example of this idea's expression is a series of comics that were used in magazine advertisements for national food brands. Most of the comics were supposed to be dramatic ("Oh, Aunt Sally, I just can't make a digestible pie crust! And John is bringing his boss home for dinner tonight!"), and their entertainment value was incidental.

31. Success Editor for newspaper, to conduct a daily column base upon the material in the eight volumes of the Law of Success, though a working alliance with the author of the Law of Success.

No single editor ever embraced this idea, but Dr. Hill did later write nationally syndicated newspaper columns.

32. Removable feet for hosiery, made of an absorbent material which will keep the feet free from perspiration, this adding to the life of the hosiery and the health and comfort of the wearer.

We now regard socks and stockings as essentially disposable items, due to decreases in the price of materials.

There is a long list of products available for coping with foot perspiration.

33. Reversible neck ties, made of two sorts of material, this giving the service of two different ties.

No one seems to have found a practical way of accomplishing this while making a tie that does not hang limply around the neck.

34. Special sets for men, consisting of shirt, tie, hose, and handkerchief to match, to be packed in a neat box, and sold at popular prices.

This idea seems to have caught on in other ways, such as coordinating sets of accessories (cufflinks and tie clip, etc.), but no retailer or manufacturer seems to have made a successful go of the fuller ensemble.

35. Elastic band fastened to the top of trousers (on the inside) this eliminating the necessity of a belt or suspenders.

This is exactly what the Sans-a-belt brand of pants does. The idea has also been applied to women's skirts, and to hospital scrubs.

36. Daily menu made up of health foods, to be syndicated in newspapers.

This idea might be more practical as a weekly feature, allowing people to plan their shopping better. Many cookbooks do provide menu plans, though not for an entire year.

37. Physical Culture Club where exercise is given through properly designed dances, thus making

physical exercise a pleasure instead of a torture.

While it might be going too far to call Napoleon Hill the father of aerobics, this is an uncanny glimpse into the future.

38. A Sales Service Agency, to be conducted by telephone, providing real estate dealers, automobile dealers, or any other business, with properly qualified prospective purchasers. (This plan may be conducted in any city, and it has unlimited possibilities for the person who understands who to present a telephone preliminary sales talk.)

Here's an idea that has succeeded so thoroughly that many of us might wish it had never been hit upon: telemarketing.

39. House organs for small business firms, to be printed upon the mimeograph, at a cost much less than that of printing, in small quantities. (Note: This idea has been put into use by two young men in New York City, and they are prepared to supply all the copy and other material necessary for others who wish to carry out a similar business in other cities. They have copy suitable for practically all sorts of businesses, such as banks, life insurance, real estate, retail stores, etc. Their names will be supplied to interested persons upon application to the author of this book.)

Part of this idea is still going strong. Employee newsletters, as they are now called, do not draw on full-service organizations such as Dr. Hill describes, in part because in-house printing is so easily accomplished. There are, however, several subscription services which provide material for people who produce these newsletters, including short articles, book reviews, and inspiring quotations that can be used as needed. What became of the young men Dr. Hill was helping by promoting their cause is unknown.

40. Organize Success Classes in business houses for the purpose of teaching the employees how to apply the Law of Success philosophy in their respective positions, to the end that both they and their employers may profit...

Motivational seminars take place daily now, offered by speakers with nearly every kind of philosophical bent, though many of them do draw on the ideas that Dr. Hill laid out in his writing. These seminars are offered not only to businesses, but to employees of the government and non-profit organizations. Even high schools offer such seminars to student leaders in the hopes of preparing them for the wider world.

These ideas hardly represent the limits of what creative thinking, used in a Master Mind situation, can suggest to you. These ideas hardly represent the limits of what can be accomplished by someone with a definite chief aim. In truth, the only limits on the power of your mind is expressed in Dr. Hill's favorite adage:

What your mind can conceive and believe,
you can achieve.

Afterword

Do you see yourself differently now? Do you see the world differently?

In truth, both are fundamentally the same as when you began reading–except that you understand how one can change the other.

This book preserves so many of Dr. Hill's examples from the past for the purpose of illustrating the unpredictable ways in which practices that first seemed immutable have altered. Men who were famous have sunk into obscurity. Everyday habits have vanished. Great corporations have come and gone. Buildings have risen and fallen.

All these changes took place, not by chance but, for better or worse, by human ingenuity. The dreams in the minds of many people, transmuted into a burning desire and expressed through definite action, have made the world very different from the days in which Napoleon Hill banged out a manuscript on a typewriter.

The world will continue to change. Most people will be swept along by those changes, never even stopping to think that they, too, could be creating the changes that affect their lives. Transformed by what you have read, the least you can settle for now is being aware that other people are changing the world while you are not.

But there is no reason to settle for that.

There is every reason to have a burning desire to do more.

The beginnings of that burning desire are inside you.

Fan that ember of desire into something more potent, something that consumes your fear and hesitation and fuels your dreams. Use the power of that fire to move yourself to action in accord with the ideas you have learned here.

You are ready to create success.

What are you waiting for?

For additional information about any of the Napoleon Hill products, please contact the following locations:

Napoleon Hill World Learning Center
Purdue University Calumet
2300 173rd Street
Hammond, Indiana 46323-2094
Judith Williamson, Director
Uriel "Chino" Martinez, Assistant/Graphic Designer
Telephone: 219-989-3173 or 219-989-3166
Email: nhf@calumet.purdue.edu

Napoleon Hill Foundation
University of Virginia-Wise
College Relations Apt. C
1 College Avenue
Wise, VA 24293
Don Green, Executive Director
Annedia Sturgill, Assistant
Telephone: 276-328-6700 or 276-328-8753
Email: napoleonhill@uvawise.edu

Website: www.naphill.org